ESTATE PUBL

ROYAL TUNBRIDGE
TONBRIDGE SOUTHBORO
CROWBOROUGH · EDENBRIDGE etc.

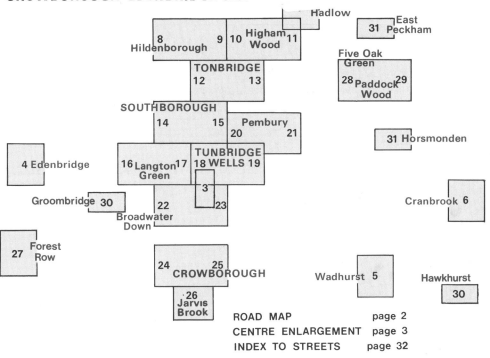

Hadlow

8 Hildenborough	9	10	Higham Wood 11	

East
31 Peckham

Five Oak Green
28 Paddock 29 Wood

TONBRIDGE
12   13

SOUTHBOROUGH
14   15   Pembury
          20   21

31 Horsmonden

4 Edenbridge   16 Langton 17   18 WELLS 19   TUNBRIDGE

3

Groombridge 30   22   23
Broadwater Down

Cranbrook 6

27 Forest Row

24   25
CROWBOROUGH

Wadhurst 5

Hawkhurst
30

· 26
Jarvis Brook

ROAD MAP   page 2
CENTRE ENLARGEMENT   page 3
INDEX TO STREETS   page 32

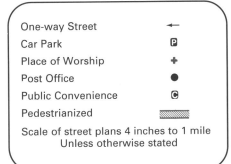

One-way Street	←
Car Park	🅿
Place of Worship	✛
Post Office	●
Public Convenience	⒞
Pedestrianized	▨▨▨

Scale of street plans 4 inches to 1 mile
Unless otherwise stated

Street plans prepared and published by ESTATE PUBLICATIONS, Bridewell House, TENTERDEN, KENT, and based upon the ORDNANCE SURVEY maps with the sanction of the Controller of H. M. Stationery Office.

The publishers acknowledge the co-operation of Tunbridge Wells B.C., Wealden D.C., and Tonbridge & Malling B.C. in the preparation of these maps.

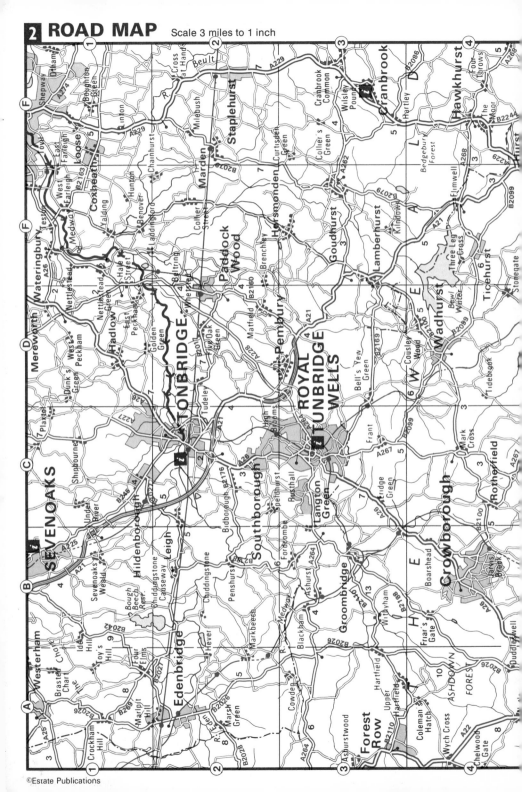

ROAD MAP

Scale 3 miles to 1 inch

©Estate Publications

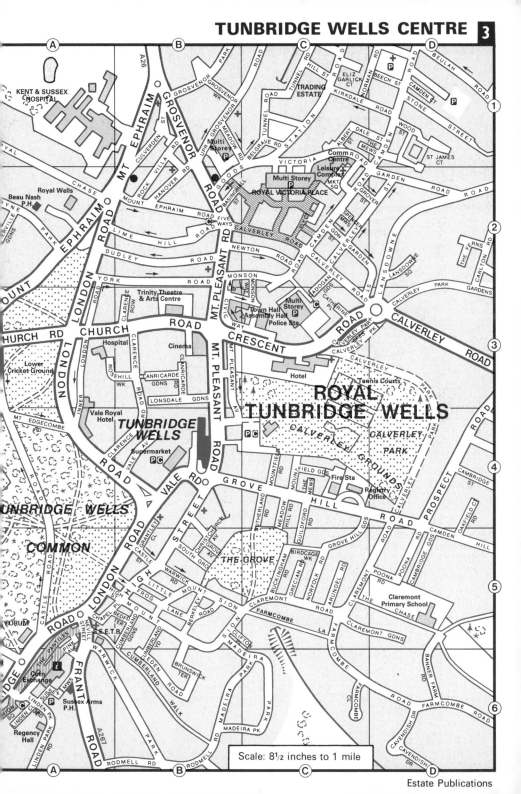

Scale: 8½ inches to 1 mile

Estate Publications

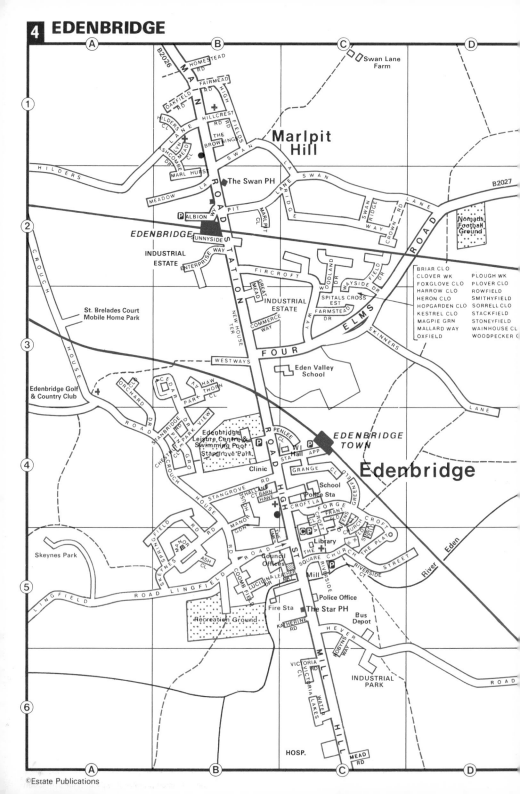

Marlpit Hill

Edenbridge

EDENBRIDGE TOWN

The Swan PH

St. Brelades Court Mobile Home Park

Edenbridge Golf & Country Club

Eden Valley School

Edenbridge Leisure Centre & Swimming Pool

Stangrove Park

Clinic

Town Hall

School

Police Sta

Library

Council Offices

Skeynes Park

Recreation Ground

Fire Sta

The Star PH

Police Office

Bus Depot

INDUSTRIAL PARK

HOSP.

Swan Lane Farm

Nomads Football Ground

INDUSTRIAL ESTATE

Industrial Estate

Spitals Cross Est

BRIAR CLO
CLOVER WK
FOXGLOVE CLO
HARROW CLO
HERON CLO
HOPGARDEN CLO
KESTREL CLO
MAGPIE GRN
MALLARD WAY
OXFIELD

PLOUGH WK
PLOVER CLO
ROWFIELD
SMITHYFIELD
SORRELL CLO
STACKFIELD
STONEYFIELD
WAINHOUSE CL
WOODPECKER C

River Eden

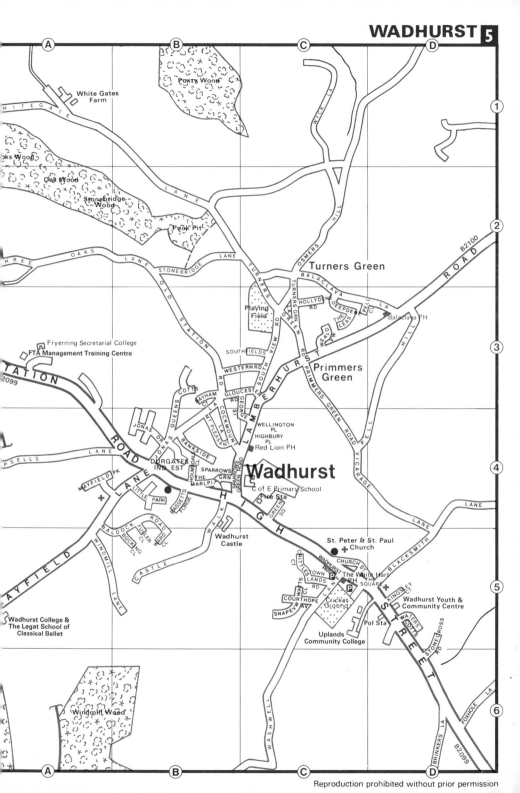

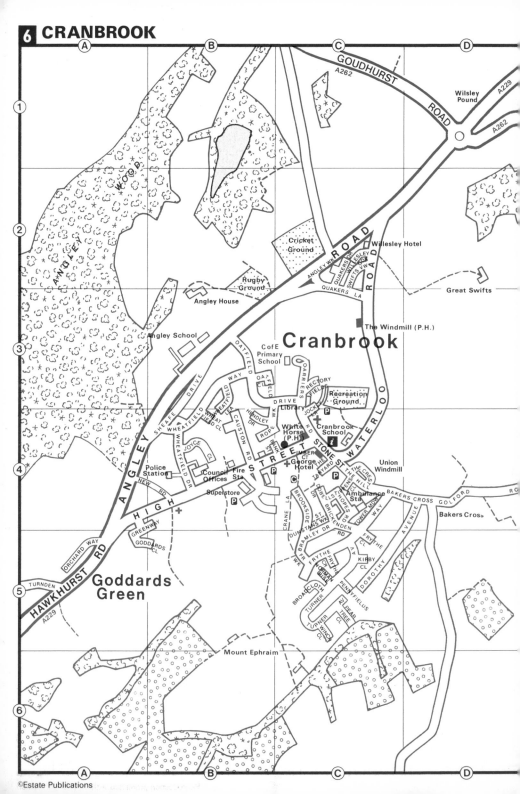

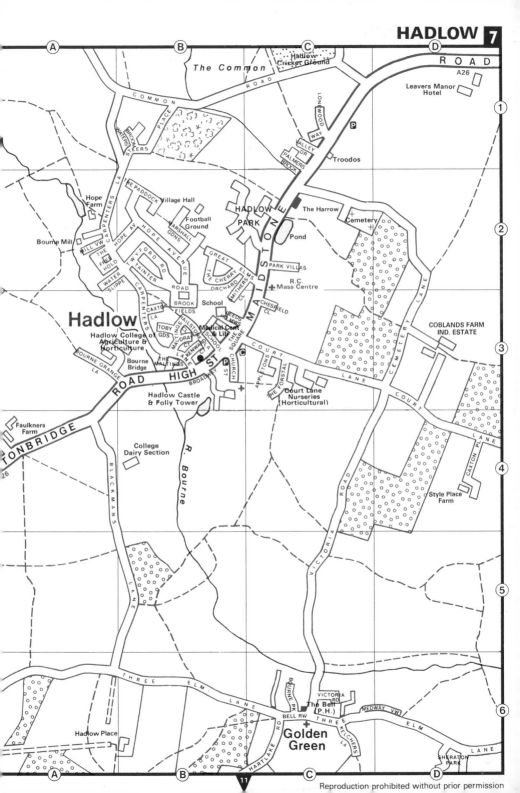

Hildenboroug

HILDENBOROUGH

Bassett's Toll

Bourne Place Wood

Flat Wood

Police Office

Church Hall

Primary Sch

Sports Grd

Riding Park

The Raphael Medical Centre

HARDWICK RD

DERBY CL

Village Hall

Library

Ringshill Wood

Sackville School

Half Moon PH

Medical Centre

West Wood

Flying Dutchman (P.H.)

WOODFIELD AV

Golf Course

GREEN ROAD

STOCKS

The Old Barn

Stocks Green Primary Sch

FAIRFIELD

MEADWAY

WOOL

ASHLEY ROAD

WEALDEN CRES

BRAMBLE CL

BYRNESIDE

LEYBANK

BROOKMEAD

GLEN VIEW CRES

BIRCH CL

LEIGH ROAD

BY-PASS

TONBRIDGE

WATTS CROSS ROAD

NOBLE TREE ROAD

LONDON ROAD

B245

MILL LANE

RIDING LANE

GARLANDS LANE

COLDH... LANE

MOUNT PLEASANT

KNOWSLEY WAY

HARBOUR

FRANCISO RD

TONBRIDGE ROAD

LEIGH RD

FELLOWES WAY

WILSON CL

FIR TREE CL

TOPSE... RD

RINGS HILL

A21

B2027

FOXBUSH

RIDING CT RAN...

CHURCH RAN...

MOON HALL

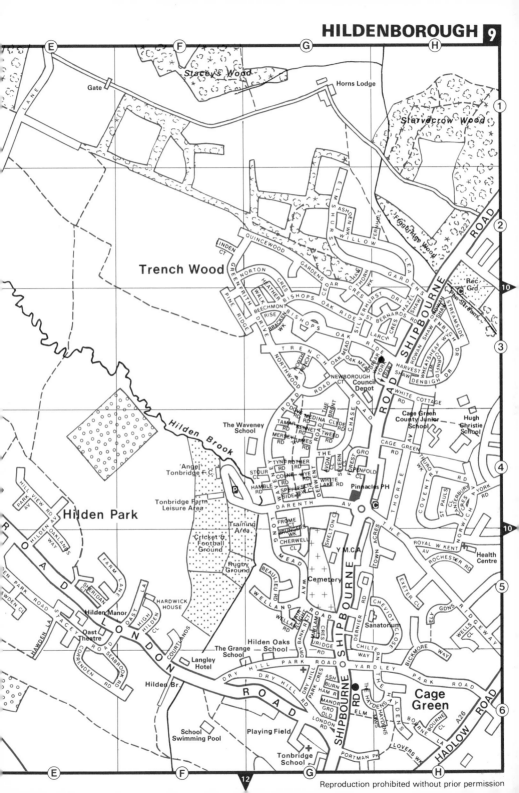

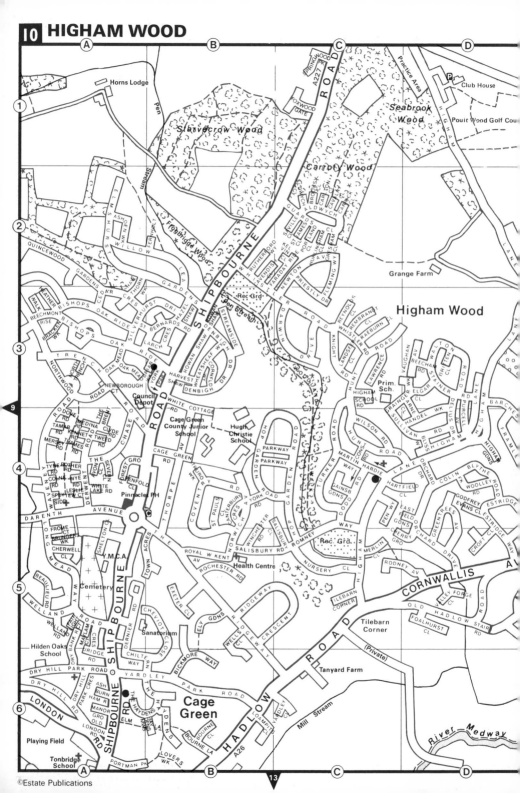

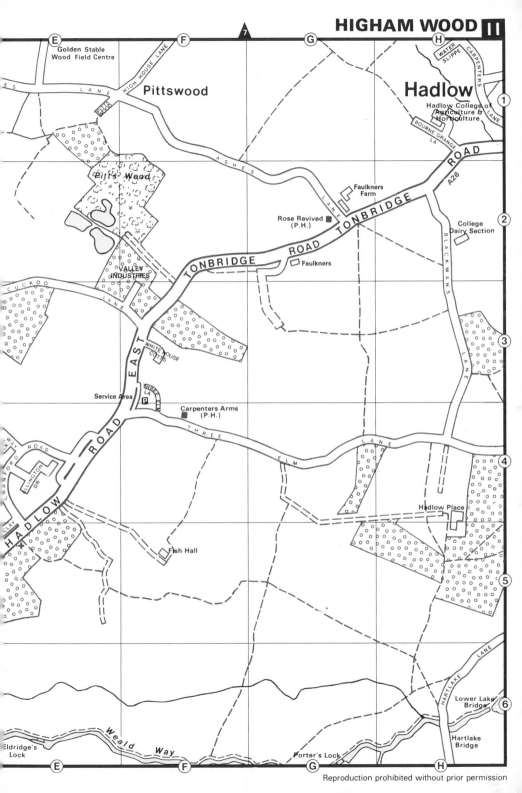

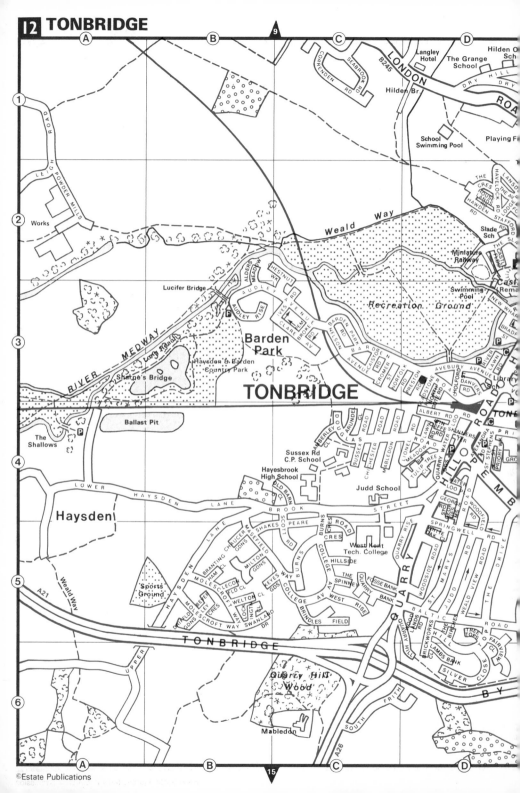

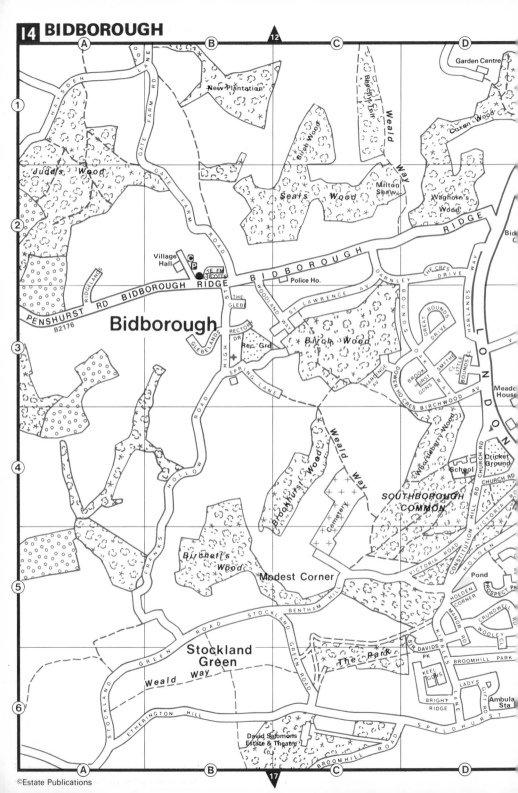

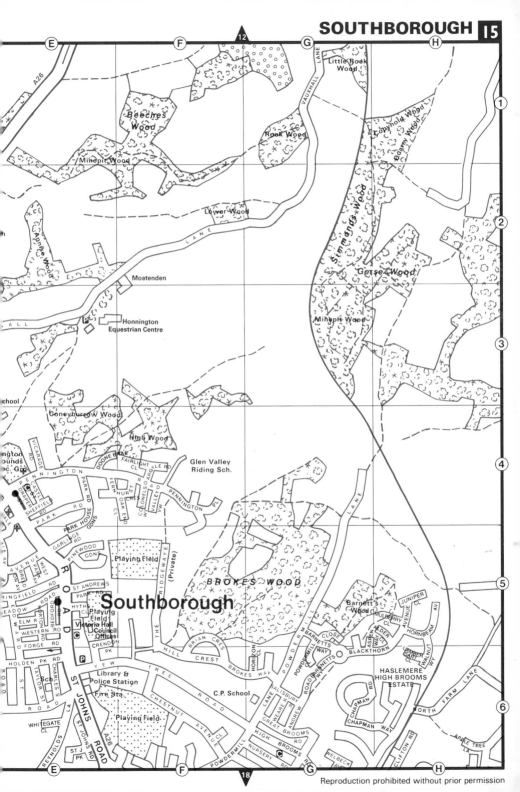

Southborough

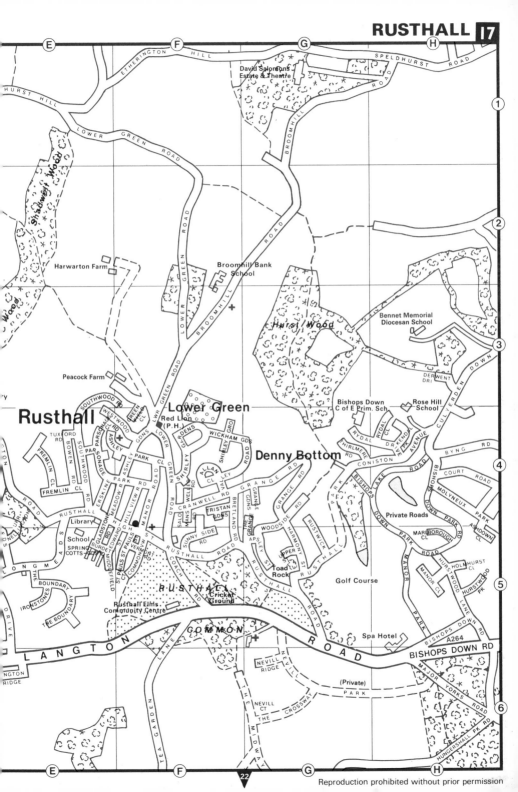

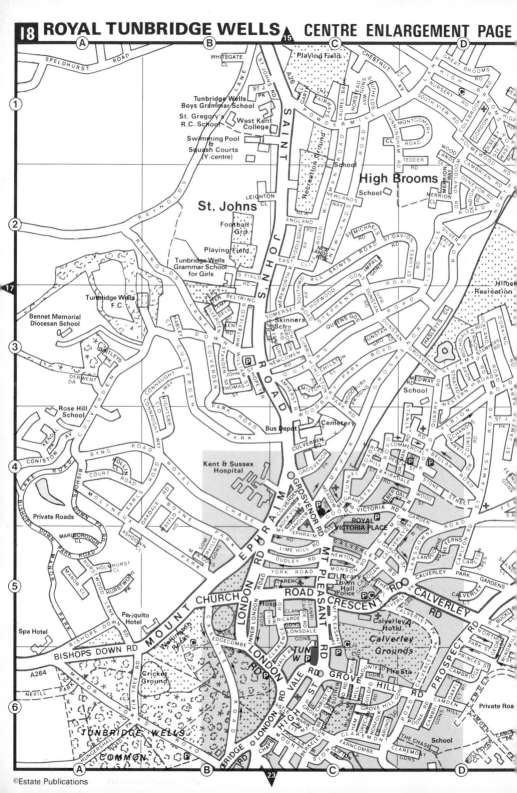

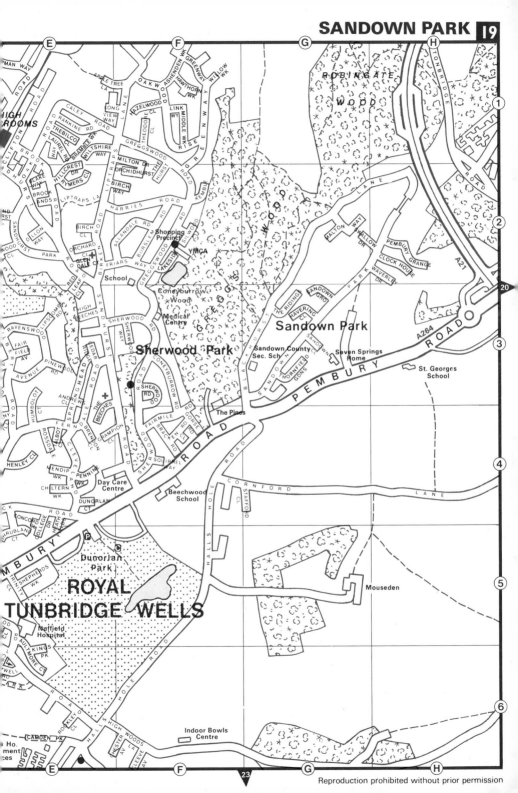

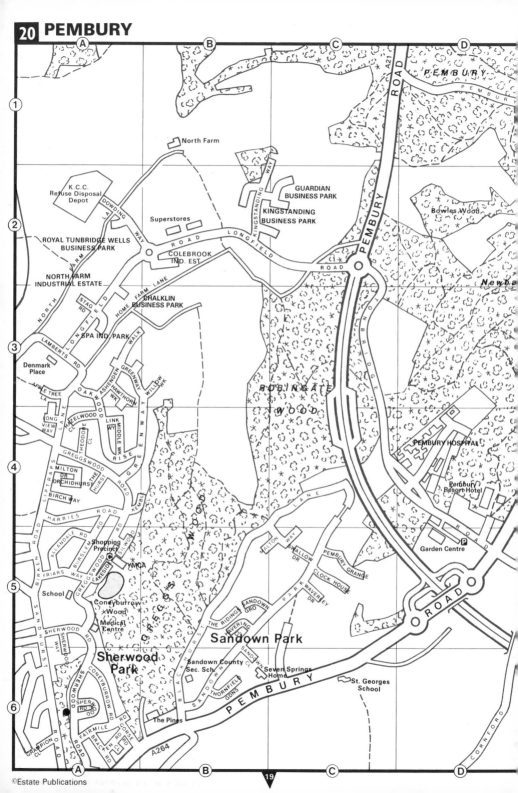

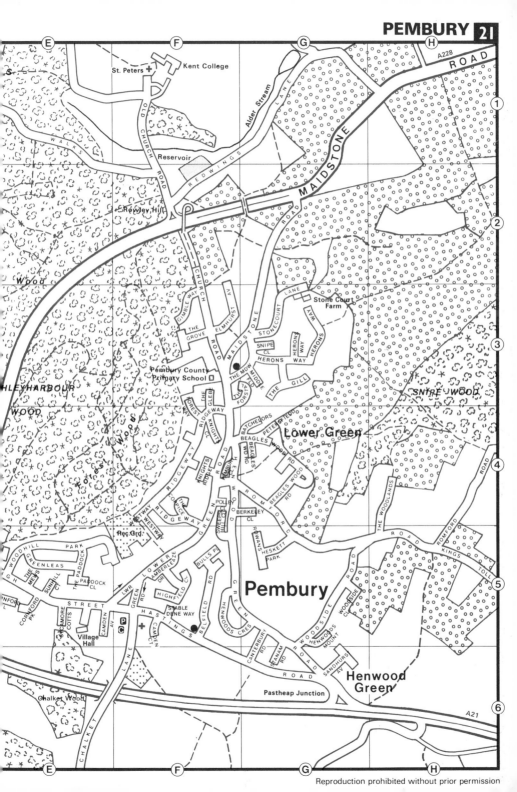

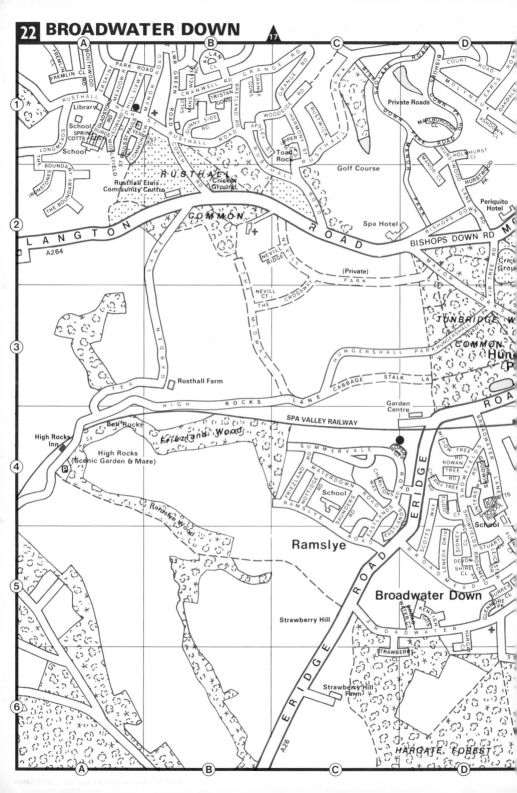

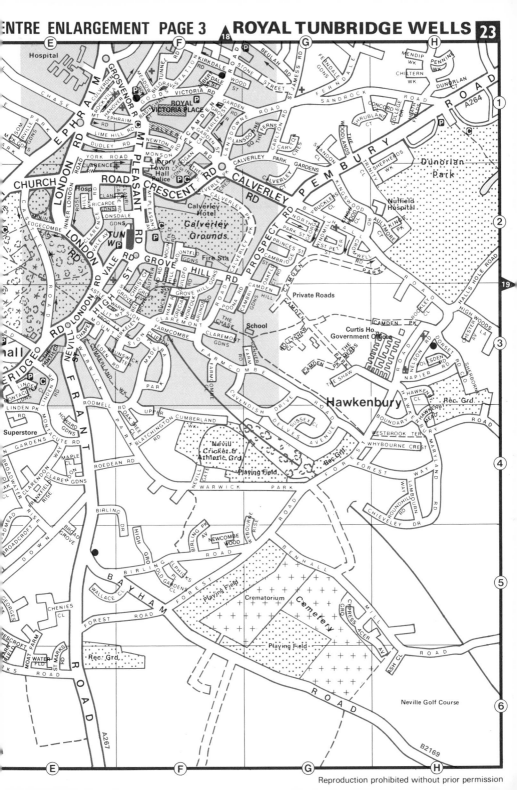

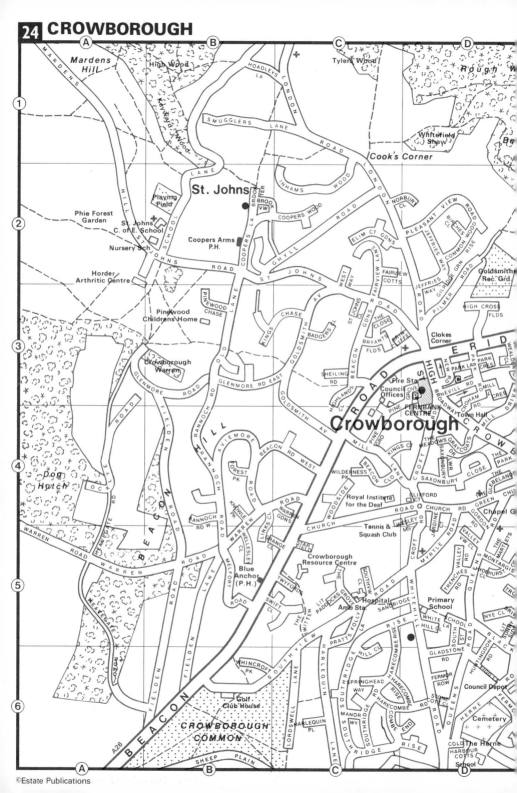

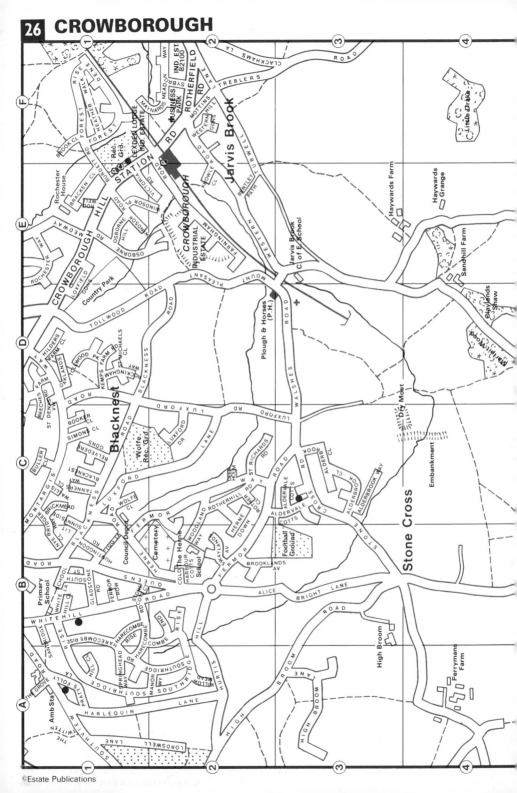

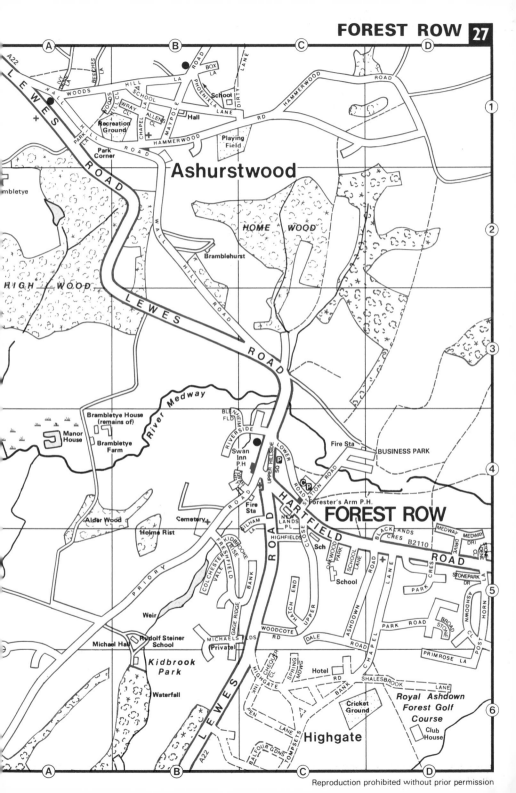

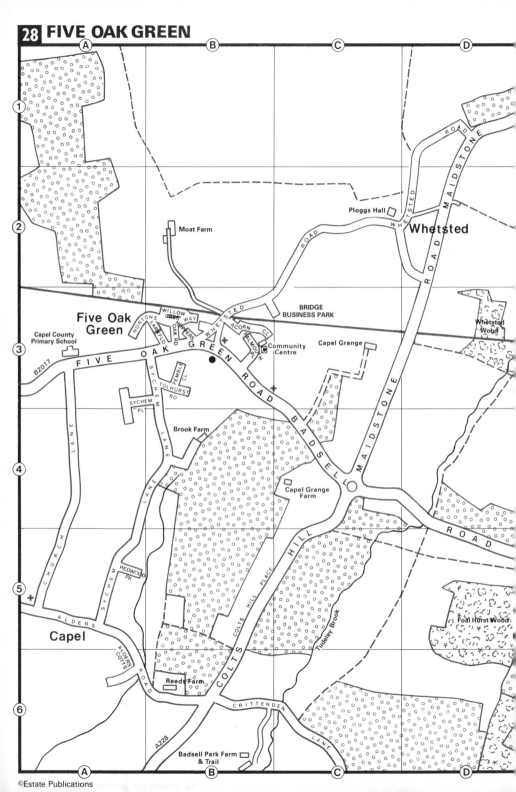

Whetsted

Ploggs Hall

Moat Farm

BRIDGE
BUSINESS PARK

Five Oak Green

Capel County
Primary School

WILLOW WAY

NORTONS

LARKFIELD

OAK RD

PEPPERS

WHETSTED

ACORN

KILMWORTH

CL

Community
Centre

Capel Grange

Whetsted
Wood

B2017

FIVE OAK GREEN ROAD

PEMBLE CL

TOLHURST RD

SYCHEM LANE

SYCHEM PLT

Brook Farm

Capel Grange
Farm

BADSELL

MAIDSTONE ROAD

CHURCH LANE

SYCHEM LANE

REDWOOD PK

Capel

ALDERS

ALDERS COTTS

COLTS HILL

COLTS HILL PLACE

Tudeley Brook

Foal Hurst Wood

Reeds Farm

ROAD

CRITTENDEN LANE

A228

Badsell Park Farm
& Trail

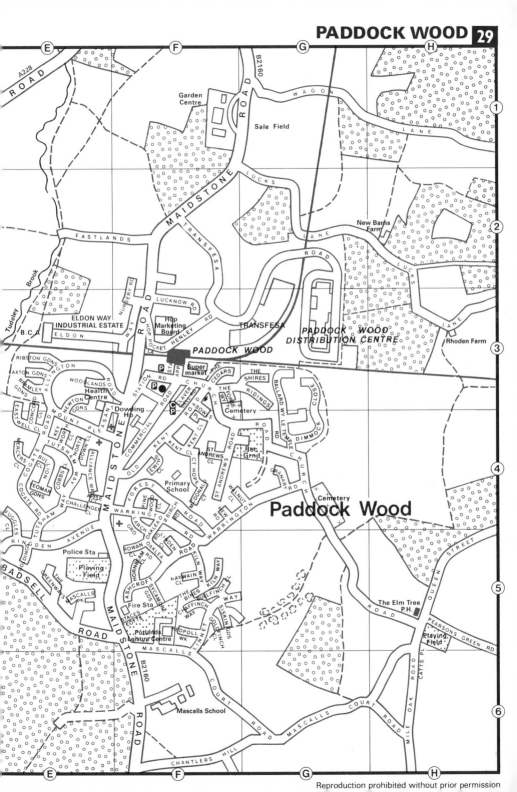

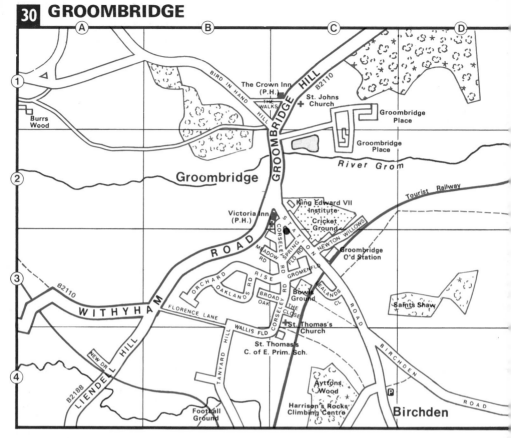

HAWKHURST

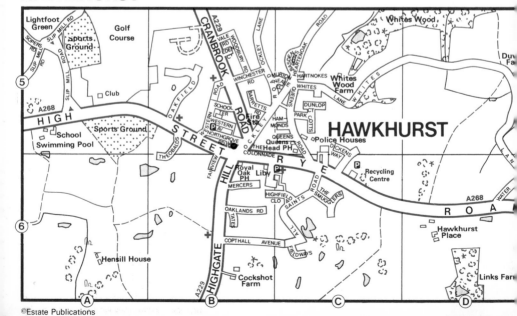

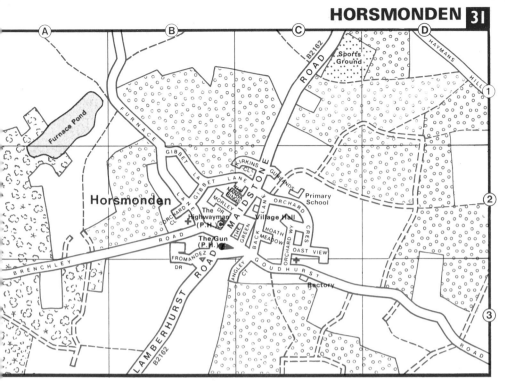

EAST PECKHAM

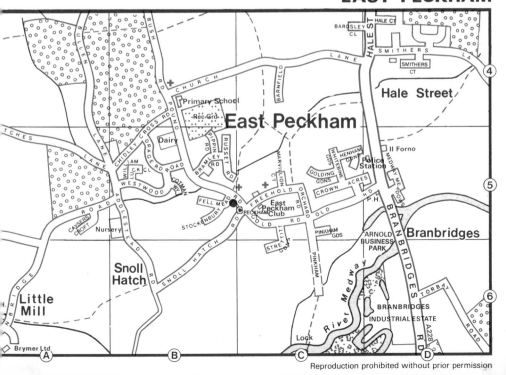

The Index includes some names for which there is insufficient space on the maps. These names are preceded by an * and are followed by the nearest adjoining thoroughfare.

TONBRIDGE

Albany Clo. TN9 — 13 F5
Albert Rd. TN9 — 12 D4
Alders Meadow. TN9 — 12 B2
Aldwych. TN10 — 10 C2
Aldwych Clo. TN10 — 10 C2
Alexandra Rd. TN9 — 12 D4
Allington Dri. TN9 — 11 E4
Amberley Clo. TN9 — 12 C4
Angel La. TN9 — 12 D3
Angel Wk. TN9 — 12 D3
Appletons. TN11 — 7 C3
Arne Clo. TN10 — 10 D3
Arundel Clo. TN9 — 12 C4
Ashburnham Rd. TN10 — 9 G6
Ashden Walk. TN10 — 9 G2
Ashes La. TN11 — 11 E1
Ashley Rd. TN11 — 8 D4
Audley Av. TN9 — 12 B3
Audley Rise. TN9 — 12 B3
Avebury Av. TN9 — 12 D3
Avenue du Puy. TN9 — 13 E4
Avon Clo. TN10 — 9 G4

Baltic Rd. TN9 — 12 D5
Bank St. TN9 — 13 E2
Barchester Way. TN10 — 10 D3
Barclay Av. TN10 — 11 E5
Barden Park Rd. TN9 — 12 C3
Barden Rd. TN9 — 12 C3
Beaulieu Rd. TN10 — 9 G5
Beecham Rd. TN10 — 10 D3
Beechmont Rise. TN10 — 9 G3
Bell Row. TN11 — 7 C6
Beverley Cres. TN9 — 12 B5
Bickmore Way. TN9 — 9 H6
Birch Clo. TN11 — 8 C5
Bishops Oak Ride. TN9 — 9 G3
Blackmans La. TN11 — 7 A4
Bliss Way. TN10 — 10 D4
Bordyke. TN9 — 13 E2
Botany. TN9 — 13 E3
Botany Ind Est. TN9 — 13 F3
Bourne Clo. TN9 — 10 B6
Bourne Grange La. TN11 — 7 A3
Bourne La. TN9 — 10 B6
Bourne Park. TN11 — 7 C6
Bracken Walk. TN10 — 9 G3
Bradford St. TN9 — 12 D3
Bramble Clo. TN11 — 8 D5
Brantingham Clo. TN9 — 12 B5
Briar Walk. TN10 — 9 H3
Brickworks Clo. TN9 — 12 C5
Bridge Clo. TN9 — 13 E4
Brindles Field. TN9 — 12 C5
Brionne Gdns. TN9 — 13 F4
Britten Clo. TN10 — 10 D3
Brook La. TN9 — 13 F2
Brook St. TN9 — 12 C4
Brookfields. TN11 — 7 B3
Brookmead. TN11 — 8 C5
Brooks Clo. TN10 — 10 C2
Broom Waters. TN11 — 7 B1
Brungers Walk. TN10 — 9 G5
Burns Cres. TN9 — 12 C5
Byrneside. TN11 — 8 D5

Cage Green Rd. TN10 — 10 B4
Caistor Rd. TN9 — 12 C3
Cannon Bridge Works. TN9 — 13 F2
Cannon La. TN9 — 13 F2
Canterbury Cres. TN10 — 10 B4
Cardinal Clo. TN9 — 13 F5
Carlton Clo. TN10 — 10 C2
Carpenters La. TN11 — 7 B2
Carrick Clo. TN10 — 10 C2
Castle Fields. TN9 — 12 D2
Castle St. TN9 — 13 E2
Cavalry Clo. TN10 — 10 C2
Cavendish Clo. TN10 — 10 B2
Caxton Clo. TN11 — 7 B3
Caxton Pl. TN11 — 7 D4

Cedar Cres. TN10 — 9 G2
Cemetary La. TN11 — 7 D3
Charlton Ter. TN9 — 13 E2
Chaucer Gdns. TN9 — 12 B5
Cherry Gro. TN10 — 10 C5
Cherwell Clo. TN10 — 9 G5
Chesfield Clo. TN11 — 7 C3
Chestnut Walk. TN9 — 12 C2
Cheviot Clo. TN9 — 10 B5
Chichester Rd. TN9 — 12 C4
Chiltern Way. TN9 — 10 A6
Church La. TN9 — 13 E2
Church Rd. TN11 — 8 C3
Church St, Hadlow. TN11 — 7 B3
Church St, Tonbridge. TN9 — 13 E2
Clare Av. TN9 — 12 C3
Clyde Rd. TN9 — 9 G4
Coblands Farm Ind Est. TN11 — 7 D3
Coldharbour La. TN11 — 8 C3
Colin Blythe Rd. TN10 — 10 D4
College Av. TN9 — 12 C5
Colne Rd. TN9 — 9 G4
Commercial Rd. TN9 — 13 E4
Common Rd. TN11 — 7 B1
Constable Rd. TN10 — 10 C4
Copse Rd. TN11 — 8 D5
Cornfield Way. TN10 — 10 B3
Cornwallis Av. TN10 — 10 D5
Correnden Rd. TN10 — 9 E6
Court La. TN11 — 7 C3
Courtlands. TN10 — 9 F5
Coventry Rd. TN10 — 10 B4
Cranford Rd. TN10 — 11 E4
Croft Clo. TN10 — 10 D5
Cromer St. TN9 — 12 C3
Cuckoo La. TN11 — 11 E3

Danvers Rd. TN10 — 12 D3
Darenth Av. TN10 — 9 G4
Darwin Dri. TN10 — 10 C3
Deacon Trading Est. TN9 — 13 F3
Deakin Leas. TN9 — 12 D6
Delius Dri. TN10 — 10 D3
Denbigh Dri. TN10 — 10 B3
Derby Clo. TN11 — 8 C3
Dernier Rd. TN10 — 10 A5
Derwent Rd. TN10 — 10 C4
Dodd Rd. TN10 — 10 C4
Douglas Rd. TN9 — 12 C4
Dove Rd. TN10 — 9 G4
Dowgate Clo. TN9 — 13 F5
Dray Ct. TN11 — 7 B3
Drayton Rd. TN9 — 13 E4
Driffield Gdns. TN9 — 12 B5
Dry Bank Rd. TN10 — 10 C3
Dry Hill Park Cres. TN10 — 9 G6
Dry Hill Park Rd. TN10 — 9 G6
Dry Hill Rd. TN9 — 9 G6

East St. TN9 — 13 E2
Eastfield Gdns. TN10 — 10 D4
Elgar Clo. TN10 — 10 D3
Elm Gro. TN11 — 8 D5
Elm La. TN10 — 9 G6
Elmshurst Gdns. TN10 — 9 G2
Ely Gdns. TN10 — 10 B5
Estridge Way. TN10 — 10 D4
Exeter Clo. TN10 — 10 B5

Fairfield Cres. TN9 — 13 E5
Fairfield Way. TN11 — 8 D4
Fairlight Ct. TN10 — 9 G5
Fairview Clo. TN9 — 12 D5
Faraday Ride. TN10 — 10 B2
Farm La. TN10 — 9 E5
Fellowes Way. TN11 — 8 D4
Fernholt. TN10 — 9 H2
Fir Tree Clo. 11 — 8 D4
Five Oak Green Rd. TN11 — 13 G5
Fleming Way. TN10 — 10 C5
Foalhurst Clo. TN10 — 10 D5
Forest Gro. TN10 — 9 G4
Fosse Bank Clo. TN9 — 12 C5
Fosse Rd. TN9 — 12 D2
Foxbush. TN11 — 8 B2
Foxwood Gate. TN11 — 10 C1
Framley Rd. TN10 — 10 D4
Francis Rd. TN10 — 8 C3
Frank Woolley Rd. TN10 — 10 D4
Frome Ct. TN10 — 9 G4

Gainsborough Gdns. TN10 — 10 C4
Garden Rd. TN9 — 13 E2
*Gardyne Mews, Springwell Rd. TN9 — 12 D4
Garlands. TN11 — 8 C1
George Rd. TN9 — 12 D4
Gladstone Rd. TN9 — 12 D3
Godfrey Evans Clo. TN10 — 10 D4
Goldsmid Rd. TN9 — 13 E4
Gorham Dri. TN9 — 13 G4
Grainger Walk. TN10 — 10 C3
Great Elms. TN11 — 7 B2
Green Frith Dri. TN9 — 9 G2
Greentrees Av. TN10 — 10 D4
Greenview Cres. TN11 — 8 C5
Gresham Clo. TN10 — 10 C2
Guards Clo. TN10 — 10 C2
Guestwick. TN10 — 10 D4

Hadlow Park. TN11 — 7 C2
Hadlow Rd. TN9 — 10 B6
Hadlow Rd East. TN11 — 11 E5
Hadlow Stair. TN10 — 10 D5
Hailstone Clo. TN11 — 7 B3
Half Moon La. TN11 — 8 C3
Hamble Rd. TN10 — 9 G4
Handel Walk. TN10 — 10 D3
Hardwick House. TN10 — 9 F5
Hardwick Rd. TN11 — 8 C2
Hartfield Clo. TN10 — 10 C4
Hartlake Rd. TN11 — 11 H6
Harvest Shaw. TN10 — 10 B3
Havelock Rd. TN9 — 12 D2
Hawden Clo. TN11 — 9 E5
Hawden La. TN11 — 9 E5
Hawden Rd. TN9 — 12 D2
Hawthorn Walk. TN10 — 9 G2
Haydens Mws. TN9 — 9 H6
Hazelshaw. TN10 — 9 H3
Heather Walk. TN10 — 9 G3
Hectorage Rd. TN9 — 13 E4
High Hilden Clo. TN10 — 9 G2
High House La. TN11 — 11 F1
High St. TN11 — 7 B3
High St. TN9 — 13 E3
Higham Gro. TN10 — 10 D4
Higham La. TN10 — 10 D1
Higham School Rd. TN10 — 10 C3
Hilden Av. TN11 — 9 E4
Hilden Park Rd. TN11 — 9 E5
Hill Rd. TN9 — 12 D4
Hill Top. TN9 — 12 D5
Hill View Rd. TN11 — 9 E4
Hillside. TN9 — 12 C5
Holford St. TN9 — 12 D3
Hop Garden Rd. TN10 — 10 B4
Hope Av. TN9 — 7 B2
Houselands Rd. TN9 — 12 D2
Hunt Rd. TN10 — 10 C4
Hurlingham Clo. TN10 — 10 C2

INDUSTRIAL ESTATES:
Botany Ind Est. TN9 — 13 F3
Coblands Farm Ind Est. TN11 — 7 D3
Deacon Trading Est. TN9 — 13 F3
Munday Works Est. TN9 — 13 E3
Orchard Business Centre. TN9 — 13 F3
Sovereign Way Ind Est. TN9 — 13 F3
Valley Industries. TN10 — 11 F3
Ives Rd. TN9 — 12 C3

Judd Rd. TN9 — 12 D5

Kelchers La. TN11 — 7 C6
Kelvin Clo. TN10 — 10 C2
Kendal Dri. TN10 — 13 E2
Kennet Rd. TN10 — 9 G4
Kenward Ct. TN11 — 7 B3
Keswick Clo. TN9 — 13 E2
Keyes Gdns. TN9 — 12 B5
Kings Rd. TN9 — 13 E5
Kinnings Row. TN9 — 13 E2
Knight Rd. TN10 — 10 C3
Knowsley Way. TN10 — 8 C3

Lambs Bank. TN9 — 12 D6
Landseer Clo. TN10 — 10 C3
Lansdowne Rd. TN9 — 12 D2
Larch Cres. TN10 — 9 H3
Lavender Hill. TN9 — 13 E4
Lawn Rd. TN9 — 12 D4
Lawrence Rd. TN10 — 10 C3
Leconfield Clo. TN9 — 12 B5
Leeds House Mws. TN11 — 7 B3
Leigh Rd. TN11 — 8 D4
Leslie Tew Ct. TN10 — 9 G4
Leybank. TN11 — 8 D5
Lime Tree Clo. TN9 — 13 E2
Linden Ct. TN10 — 9 F2
Lionel Rd. TN9 — 12 D4
Loampits Clo. TN10 — 10 B6
Lockington Clo. TN9 — 12 B5
Lockside. TN9 — 13 E2
Lodge Oak La. TN10 — 13 F4
Lodge Rd. TN9 — 12 D2
London Rd. TN10 — 8 A1
Lonewood Way. TN11 — 7 C1
Long Mead Way. TN10 — 9 G4
Lovers Walk. TN10 — 9 H6
Lower Hayesden La. TN11 — 12 A4
Lyons Cres. TN9 — 13 E3

Mabledon Rd. TN9 — 12 C4
Magnolia Clo. TN9 — 13 E6
Maidstone Rd. TN11 — 7 C3
Maltings Clo. TN11 — 7 B3
Mann Sq. TN9 — 13 F5
Manor Gro. TN10 — 9 G6
Marshall Gdns. TN11 — 7 B2
Martin Hardie Way. TN10 — 10 C4
Mary Magdalene Ho. TN9 — 12 D4
Masefield Way. TN9 — 12 B5
Maylam Ct. TN10 — 9 G5
Meadow Rd. TN9 — 12 D4
Meadway. TN11 — 8 D4
Medina Rd. TN10 — 9 G4
Medway View. TN11 — 7 C6
Medway Wharf Rd. TN9 — 13 E3
Merlin Clo. TN10 — 10 C5
Mersey Rd. TN10 — 9 G4
Mill Cres. TN9 — 13 E2
Mill La. TN11 — 8 A1
Mill La. TN9 — 13 E2
Mill View. TN11 — 7 A2
Milton Gdns. TN9 — 12 B5
Mitre Ct. TN9 — 13 E2
Molescroft Way. TN9 — 12 D4
Morley Rd. TN9 — 13 F3
Mount Pleasant. TN11 — 8 C3
Mount Pleasant Ct. TN11 — 8 C3
Mountfield Park. TN9 — 12 D5
Munday Works Est. TN9 — 13 E3

Nelson Av. TN9 — 12 C3
New Ct. TN9 — 13 E2
New Wharf Rd. TN9 — 12 D3
Newborough Ct. TN9 — 9 G3
Newton Av. TN10 — 10 C2
Noble Tree Rd. TN11 — 8 A3
Norfolk Rd. TN9 — 12 B5
North Trench. TN10 — 9 G3
Northcote Rd. TN9 — 12 D3
Northwood Rd. TN10 — 9 G3
Norton Cres. TN10 — 9 G2
Norwich Av. TN10 — 10 B5
Nursery Clo. TN10 — 10 C5

Oaklands Way. TN11 — 9 E5
Oakmead. TN10 — 9 G3
Oast La. TN10 — 9 F5
Old Barn Clo. TN9 — 12 D3
Old Cannon Wharf. TN9 — 13 F3
Old Hadlow Rd. TN10 — 10 D5
Old London Rd. TN10 — 9 G4
Orchard Dri. TN10 — 10 D4
Orchard Lea. TN10 — 8 D4
Orchard Business Centre. TN9 — 13 F3

Palmers Brook. TN9 — 7 C1
Park Av. TN11 — 9 E4
Park Villas. TN11 — 7 C2
Parkway. TN10 — 10 B4
Pembroke Rd. TN9 — 12 C3
Pembury Gro. TN9 — 13 E4

Pembury Rd. TN9 — 12 D4
Pen Way. TN10 — 10 C4
Penfold Clo. TN10 — 9 G4
Pine Ridge. TN10 — 9 F3
Pittswood. TN11 — 11 F1
Portland Clo. TN10 — 10 D4
Portman Pk. TN9 — 13 E1
Postern La. TN11 — 13 F3
Powder Mills. TN11 — 12 A2
Preston Rd. TN9 — 12 D3
Priestley Dri. TN10 — 10 C2
Priory Gro. TN9 — 12 D4
Priory Rd. TN9 — 12 D4
Priory St. TN9 — 12 D4
Priory Walk. TN9 — 12 D4
Purcell Rd. TN10 — 10 D3

Quarry Bank. TN9 — 12 C5
Quarry Gdns. TN9 — 12 C5
Quarry Rd. TN9 — 12 C5
Quarry Hill Rd. TN9 — 12 C5
Quarry Rise. TN9 — 12 C5
Quincewood Gdns. TN10 — 9 G2

Raeburn Clo. TN10 — 10 C3
Rembrandt Clo. TN10 — 10 C3
Reynolds Clo. TN10 — 10 C3
Ridgeway Cres. TN10 — 10 B5
Riding La. TN11 — 8 C1
Riding Pk. TN11 — 8 A3
Rings Hill. TN11 — 8 A3
River Lawn. TN9 — 12 D3
River Walk. TN9 — 12 D3
Riverside Ct. TN9 — 13 E3
Rochester Rd. TN10 — 10 B5
Rodney Av. TN10 — 10 C5
Romney Way. TN10 — 10 C5
Rose St. TN9 — 13 E4
Rother Rd. TN9 — 9 G4
Rowan Shaw. TN10 — 10 B3
Royal Ave. TN10 — 13 E5
Royal West Kent Av. TN10 — 10 B5
Rutherford Way. TN10 — 10 B2

St Bernards Rd. TN10 — 9 H3
St Georges Mews. TN9 — 12 D4
St James Clo. TN10 — 10 C2
St Marys Rd. TN9 — 12 D5
St Pauls Clo. TN10 — 10 B4
St Stephens St. TN9 — 12 D4
Salisbury Clo. TN10 — 10 B4
Salisbury Rd. TN10 — 10 B5
Sanderson Way. TN9 — 13 F3
Saville Clo. TN10 — 10 C2
School La. TN11 — 7 B3
Scott Rd. TN9 — 12 C5
Seabrook Rd. TN10 — 9 E6
Severn Clo. TN10 — 9 G4
Shakespeare Rd. TN9 — 12 C5
Shelton Clo. TN9 — 9 G4
Sheraton Park. TN11 — 7 D6
Sheridan Ct. TN10 — 9 E5
Shipbourne Rd. TN10 — 10 A6
Shrublands Ct. TN9 — 13 F2
Silver Clo. TN10 — 12 D6
Silverhurst Dri. TN10 — 9 G3
Skinners Ter. TN9 — 12 D4
Smithers Clo. TN11 — 7 C2
Somerhill Rd. TN9 — 13 F4
South Frith. TN9 — 12 D3
Sovereign Way. TN9 — 13 E3
Sovereign Way Ind Est. TN9 — 13 F3
Speyside. TN10 — 9 G4
Springwell Rd. TN9 — 12 D5
Springwood Pk. TN11 — 10 C1
Stacey Rd. TN10 — 9 E5
Stafford Rd. TN9 — 12 D2
Stainer Rd. TN10 — 10 D3
Stair Rd. TN10 — 10 D5
Steers Pl. TN11 — 7 B1
Stocks Green Rd. TN11 — 8 A3
Stour Clo. TN10 — 9 G4
Strawberry Vale. TN9 — 12 D3
Streamside. TN10 — 10 B3
Sullivan Rd. TN10 — 10 D3
Sussex Rd. TN9 — 12 D4
Swanland Dri. TN10 — 12 B5
Swanmead Way. TN9 — 13 E4

Tainter Rd. TN11 — 7 B2
Tamar Rd. TN9 — 9 G4

TUNBRIDGE WELLS

Street	Ref
Hill Crest Dri. TN2	19 E1
Hill Garth. TN4	18 C1
Hill St. TN1	3 C1
Hill View Rd. TN4	17 F4
Hither Chantlers. TN3	16 D6
Holden Corner. TN4	14 D5
Holden Park Rd. TN4	15 E6
Holden Rd. TN4	14 D5
Hollin Clo. TN4	18 A4
Hollyshaw Clo. TN2	23 G3
Holmewood Ridge. TN3	16 C6
Holmewood Road. TN4	18 D1
Holmhurst Clo. TN4	18 A5
Home Farm La. TN2	20 A3
Homewood Rd. TN3	16 C5
Hope Ter. TN4	18 B3
Hopwood Gdns. TN4	18 C3
Horizon Clo. TN4	15 G6
Hornbeam Av. TN4	15 H5
Howard Gdns. TN2	23 E4
Humbolot Ct. TN2	19 E4
Hungershall Pk. TN4	22 C3
Hungershall Pk Rd. TN2	22 D3
Hunters Way. TN2	22 D4
Huntleys Pk. TN4	18 A3
Hurstwood La. TN4	18 A5
Hurstwood Park. TN4	18 A5
Hythe Clo. TN4	15 E5
Impala Gdns. TN4	18 C2
INDUSTRIAL ESTATES:	
Chalklin Business Park. TN2	20 A3
Colebrook Ind Est. TN2	20 B2
Guardian Business Park. TN2	20 C2
Haslemere High Brooms Estate. TN4	15 H6
Kingstanding Business Park. TN2	20 B2
North Farm Ind Est. TN2	20 A2
Royal Tunbridge Wells Business Park. TN2	20 A2
Spa Ind. Park. TN2	20 A3
Inner London Rd. TN1	3 A3
Ironstones. TN3	17 E5
*John Spare Ct, Whitefield Rd. TN4	18 B3
John St. TN4	18 B3
Juniper Clo. TN4	15 G5
Keel Gdns. TN4	14 D6
Kemble Clo. TN2	19 F2
Kendal Pk. TN4	17 H4
Kent Rd. TN4	18 B3
Kentish Gdns. TN2	22 D5
Kibbles La. TN4	14 D5
King George V Hill. TN2	19 E3
Kings Park. TN2	19 E5
Kings Toll. TN2	21 H5
Kingstanding Business Park. TN2	20 B2
Kingstanding Way. TN2	20 B2
Kingswood Clo. TN2	19 E5
Kingswood Rd. TN2	19 E5
Kirby Ct. TN3	16 D6
Kirkdale Rd. TN1	3 C1
Knights Clo. TN2	21 F4
Knights Pl. TN2	21 C2
Knights Ridge. TN2	21 F4
Knightsbridge Clo. TN3	18 B3
Knowle Clo. TN3	16 C5
*Laburnum Ct, Sandhurst Rd. TN2	19 E2
Lady's Gift Rd. TN4	14 D6
Lake Rd. TN4	17 H4
Lakeside. TN2	19 F2
Lambersart Clo. TN4	15 H6
Lamberts Rd. TN2	20 A3
Lambourn Way. TN2	23 H4
Lampington Row. TN3	16 B5
Langholme Rd. TN3	16 C5
Langton Ridge. TN3	17 E6
Langton Rd, Langton. TN3	17 E6
Langton Rd, Speldhurst. TN3	16 C3
Lansdowne Rd. TN1	3 D2
Lansdowne Sq. TN1	3 D2
Laurel Bank. TN4	18 C1
Laurel Rd. TN2	19 E1
Laurel Way. TN2	19 E1
Leggs La. TN3	16 A3
Leicester Dri. TN2	22 D5
Leighton Clo. TN4	18 B2
Leneda Dri. TN2	22 D5
Lime Hill Rd. TN1	3 B2
Linden Clo. TN4	3 A6
Linden Gdns. TN2	23 E4
Linden Park Rd. TN4	3 A6
Link Way. TN4	19 F1
Lipscombe Rd. TN2	19 E3
Liptraps La. TN2	19 E2
Little Bounds Clo. TN4	14 D3
Little Footway. TN3	16 C5
*Little Mallett, Third St. TN3	16 C5
Little Mount Sion. TN1	3 B5
London Rd. TN4	14 D3
London Rd. TN1	3 A3
Long Slip. TN3	16 D5
Long View Way. TN2	19 E1
Longfield Rd. TN2	20 A3
Longmeads. TN3	17 E5
Lonsdale Gdns. TN1	3 B3
Lower Green Rd. TN2	21 F5
Lower Green Rd. TN4	17 E1
Madeira Pk. TN2	3 B6
Maidstone Rd. TN2	21 G2
Major Yorks Rd. TN4	18 A6
Malton Way. TN2	20 C5
Manor Clo. TN4	18 A5
Manor Pk. TN4	18 A5
Manor Rd, Rusthall. TN4	17 F4
Manor Rd, Southborough. TN4	14 D5
Maple Clo. TN2	23 E4
Market Sq. TN1	3 C2
Market St. TN2	23 E3
Marlborough Clo. TN4	17 H5
Maryland Rd. TN2	23 H4
Mayfield Rd. TN4	18 A4
Meadow Hill Rd. TN1	3 C4
Meadow Rd, Rusthall. TN4	17 E4
Meadow Rd, Southborough. TN4	14 D5
Meadow Rd. TN1	3 B1
Medway Rd. TN1	18 D3
Mendip Walk. TN2	19 E4
Mercer St. TN1	18 C4
Mercers. TN3	16 D5
Mereworth Rd. TN4	18 C3
Merrion Clo. TN4	18 D2
Merrion Way. TN4	18 D2
Middle Walk. TN2	19 F1
Middlefield. TN2	21 G3
Middlefield. TN4	17 E5
Milton Dri. TN2	19 F1
Moat Farm. TN2	23 E6
Molyneux Park. TN4	18 A4
Molyneux Park Gdns. TN4	18 B5
Monson Rd. TN1	3 B2
Monson Way. TN1	3 C2
Montacute Gdns. TN2	23 E3
Montacute Rd. TN2	23 E4
Monteith Clo. TN3	16 D5
Montgomery Rd. TN4	18 D1
Mount Edgecombe Rd. TN1	3 A4
Mount Ephraim. TN4	3 A3
Mount Ephraim Rd. TN1	3 B2
Mount Pleasant Av. TN1	3 B3
Mount Pleasant Rd. TN1	3 B3
Mount Sion. TN1	3 B5
Mountfield Gdns. TN1	3 C4
Mountfield Rd. TN1	3 C4
Mulberry Clo. TN4	15 H5
Napier Rd. TN2	23 H3
Nellington Rd. TN4	17 E4
Nelson Rd. TN2	23 H3
Nevill Ct. TN4	17 G6
Nevill Gate. TN2	23 F4
Nevill Park. TN4	22 C2
Nevill Ridge. TN4	17 G6
Nevill St. TN2	3 A5
Nevill Ter. TN2	23 E3
New England Rd. TN4	18 C2
Newcombe Wood. TN2	23 F5
Newcomen Rd. TN4	18 C3
Newlands. TN3	16 D5
Newlands Rise. TN4	18 C2
Newlands Road.TN4	18 C2
Newlands Way. TN4	18 C2
Newton Rd. TN1	3 B2
Norfolk Rd. TN2	3 C5
Norman Rd. TN1	3 C1
Norstead Gdns. TN4	18 C1
North Farm Ind Est. TN2	20 A2
North Farm Rd. TN2	18 D2
North St. TN2	18 D5
Northfield Rd. TN3	16 D1
Norton Rd. TN4	15 E5
Nottidge Rd. TN4	22 C4
Nursery Rd. TN4	18 D1
Oak End Clo. TN4	15 F4
Oak Rd. TN2	19 E1
Oak Tree Clo. TN2	23 F4
Oakdale Rd. TN4	18 B4
Oakfield Court Rd. TN2	3 D4
Oakwood Rise. TN2	19 F1
Old Church Rd. TN2	21 F1
Old Gardens Clo. TN2	23 F5
Old House La. TN3	16 A4
Orchard Clo. TN2	19 E2
Orchidhurst. TN2	19 F2
Ox Lea. TN3	16 D5
Paddock Clo. TN2	21 E5
Park House Gdns. TN4	15 E4
Park Rd, Southborough. TN4	15 E4
Park Rd, Tun Wells. TN4	18 C3
Park St. TN2	18 D5
Parkwood Clo. TN2	19 E2
Parsonage Clo. TN4	17 E4
Parsonage Rd. TN4	17 E4
Pembury Clo. TN2	21 F4
Pembury Grange. TN2	19 H2
Pembury Rd. TN2	19 F3
Pembury Walks. TN2	20 D1
Pennine Walk. TN2	19 E4
Pennington Pl. TN2	15 F4
Pennington Rd. TN2	15 E4
Penshurst Rd, Bidborough. TN3	14 A3
Penshurst Rd, Speldhurst. TN3	16 D1
Percy Ter. TN4	18 B3
Petersfield. TN2	21 G4
Pinewood Gdns. TN4	15 E5
Pinewood Rd. TN2	19 E3
Pink All. TN2	3 A6
Polesden Rd. TN2	23 H3
Polley Clo. TN2	21 F4
Poona Rd. TN1	3 D5
Powdermill Clo. TN4	15 G6
Powdermill La. TN1	18 C1
Princes St. TN2	18 D6
Prospect Park. TN4	14 D5
Prospect Rd. TN4	15 F5
Prospect Rd. TN2	3 D4
Quarry Rd. TN1	18 D3
Queens Gdns. TN4	18 C3
Queens Rd. TN4	18 C3
Ramslye Rd. TN4	22 C4
Rankine Rd. TN2	19 E1
Ravenswood Av. TN4	19 E3
Rectory Dri. TN3	14 B3
Red Leaf Clo. TN2	19 E2
Redwings La. TN2	21 F2
Reynolds La. TN4	18 B2
Richardson Rd. TN4	18 C2
Riddlesdale Av. TN2	18 C2
Ridgelands. TN3	14 A3
Ridgeway. TN2	21 F4
Rochdale Rd. TN4	18 D3
Rock Villa Rd. TN1	3 B2
Rockley Clo. TN2	19 E6
Rodmell Rd. TN2	3 B6
Roedean Rd. TN2	23 E4
Romford Rd. TN2	21 H4
Roopers. TN3	16 D1
Roopers Gate. TN2	22 C4
Rose Hill Walk. TN1	3 B3
Rosecroft Park. TN3	16 D4
Rossdale. TN2	19 E4
Roundhill Rd. TN2	23 H4
Rowan Tree Rd. TN2	22 D4
Rowans. TN2	21 G3
Royal Chase. TN4	3 A1
Royal Tunbridge Wells Business Park. TN2	20 A2
Royal Victoria Pl. TN1	3 C2
Ruscombe Clo. TN4	14 D4
Rushetts. TN3	16 C5
Rusthall High St. TN4	17 E4
Rusthall Pk. TN4	17 G5
Rusthall Rd. TN4	17 F5
Rustwick. TN4	17 G5
Rydal Clo. TN4	17 H4
Rydal Dri. TN4	17 G4
Ryders. TN3	16 D5
Rymers Clo. TN2	19 E2
St Andrews Park Rd. TN4	15 E5
*St Barnabas Clo, Western Rd. TN1	18 D4
St Davids Rd. TN4	18 C2
St Georges Pk. TN2	23 E5
St James Ct. TN1	3 D1
St James Rd. TN1	18 D3
St James's Pk. TN1	18 D4
St John's Rd. TN4	18 C1
St Johns Park. TN4	15 E6
St Lawrence Av. TN4	14 C3
St Lukes Rd. TN4	18 D2
St Marks Rd. TN2	22 D6
St Marys La. TN3	16 D1
St Michaels Rd. TN4	18 C2
St Pauls Ct. TN4	17 F5
St Pauls St. TN4	17 F5
St Peter St. TN2	18 D6
*St Stephens Cotts, Stanley Rd. TN1	18 D4
Salisbury Rd. TN4	15 G6
Salisbury Rd. TN3	16 C5
Salomans Rd. TN4	17 F4
Sandhurst Av. TN2	21 G6
Sandhurst Clo. TN2	19 E2
Sandhurst Pk. TN2	19 E2
Sandhurst Rd. TN2	19 E2
Sandown Clo. TN2	20 B5
Sandown Gro. TN2	20 B5
Sandown Pk. TN2	20 B6
Sandrock Rd. TN2	19 E4
Saunders Rd. TN4	22 C4
School Rise. TN2	22 D4
Scotts Way. TN2	22 D5
Shaftesbury Rd. TN4	18 C3
Shandon Clo. TN2	18 D5
Sheffield Rd. TN4	15 E4
Shepherds Walk. TN2	19 E5
Sherbourne Clo. TN2	23 H3
Sherwood Rd. TN2	19 F3
Sherwood Way. TN2	19 F3
*Shirley Cotts, Woodbury Pk Rd. TN4	18 C4
Shirley Rd. TN4	17 F4
Shirley Gro. TN4	17 F4
Showfields Rd. TN2	22 D4
Shrubland Ct. TN2	19 E5
Sidney Clo. TN2	22 D5
Silverdale La. TN4	18 D2
Silverdale Rd. TN4	18 D2
Silwood Clo. TN2	19 F2
Sir Davids Rd. TN4	14 D5
Smythe Clo. TN4	14 D3
Snipe Clo. TN2	21 G3
Somerset Rd. TN4	18 C3
Somerville Gdns. TN4	3 A2
South Gro. TN1	3 B5
South View Rd. TN4	18 D1
Southfield Rd. TN3	16 D1
Southfield Rd. TN4	18 B2
Southfields Av. TN4	18 C1
Southwood Av. TN4	18 C3
Southwood Rd. TN3	17 E3
Spa Ind. Park. TN2	20 A3
Speldhurst Hill. TN3	17 E1
Speldhurst Rd. TN4	14 D6
Speldhurst Rd. TN3	16 B5
Spencer Mews. TN1	3 C2
Spring Cotts. TN2	17 E5
Spring Gdns. TN4	17 E5
Spring La. TN3	14 B3
Springfield Rd. TN4	15 E5
Springhead. TN2	19 E3
Squirrel Way. TN2	19 F4
Stabledene Way. TN2	21 F5
Stafford Clo. TN4	19 G4
Stag Rd. TN2	20 A3
Stanam Rd. TN2	21 G6
Standen St. TN4	18 B3
Stanhope Rd. TN1	18 D4
Stanley Rd. TN1	18 D4
Stephens Rd. TN4	18 C3
Stewart Rd. TN4	18 D1
Still La. TN4	15 E4
Stockland Green Rd. TN3	14 A6
Stone St. TN1	3 D1
Stonecourt La. TN2	21 G3
Stonewall Park Rd. TN3	16 C5
Stratford St. TN1	18 D3
Strawberry Clo. TN2	22 C5
Stuart Clo. TN2	22 D5
Summerhill Av. TN4	14 D5
Summervale Rd. TN4	22 C4
Sunhill Ct. TN2	21 E5
Sunnyside Rd. TN4	17 F5
Surrey Clo. TN2	22 D5
Sussex Clo. TN2	23 G4
Sussex Mews. TN2	3 A6
Sutherland Rd. TN1	3 C4
Swallow Dri. TN2	20 C
Sweepshill Clo. TN2	21 F
Sycamore Cotts. TN3	21 E
Talbot Clo. TN2	19 E
*Taylor Ct, Brook Rd. TN2	19 E
Taylor St. TN4	15 E
Tea Garden La. TN3	22 A
Tedder Rd. TN4	18 D
The Beeches. TN2	19 E
The Boundary. TN3	17 E
The Chase. TN1	3 D
The Close. TN2	19 E
The Coppice. TN2	21 F
The Crescent. TN4	14 D
The Crossway. TN4	22 C
The Fairways. TN2	18 C
The Ferns. TN1	3 D
The Forstal. TN2	21 G
The Forum. TN1	3 A
The Gill. TN2	21 G
The Glebe. TN3	14 B
The Glebe. TN2	21 F
The Goodwins. TN2	22 D
The Grange. TN4	17 G
The Grove. TN2	21 F
The Hurst. TN2	19 F
The Meadow. TN2	21 G
The Meads. TN2	23 G
The Mews. TN2	21 E
The Mews, Camden Rd. TN1	3 D
The Mews, Grove Hill Rd. TN1	3 C
The Midway. TN4	22 B
*The Nightingales, Queens Rd. TN4	18 C
The Paddock. TN2	21 E
The Pantiles. TN2	3 A
The Ridgewaye. TN4	15 F
The Ridings. TN2	19 G
The Shaw. TN2	23 G
The Spurway. TN4	22 B
The Woodlands, Pembury. TN2	21 H
The Woodlands, Tun Wells. TN2	19 E
Theodore Clo. TN2	19 F
Third St. TN3	16 C
Thirlmere Rd. TN4	17 G
Thomas St. TN4	18 B
Thornfield Gdns. TN2	19 G
Tonbridge Rd. TN2	20 C
Trebilco Clo. TN2	19 E
Trinity Clo. TN2	19 E
Tristan Gdns. TN4	17 F
Tudor Ct. TN2	22 D
Tunnel Rd. TN1	3 C
Tuxford Rd. TN4	17 E
Union Sq. TN4	3 A
Upper Cumberland Walk. TN2	23 F
Upper Dunstan Rd. TN4	18 C
Upper Grosvenor Rd. TN1	3 B
Upper Nellington. TN3	17 E
Upper Profit. TN3	16 D
Upper Stephens. TN3	16 D
Upper St. TN4	17 G
Upton Quarry. TN3	16 C
Vale Av. TN4	15 E
Vale Av. TN1	3 B
Vale Rd. TN4	3 B
Vale Rd. TN1	3 B
Valley Rd. TN4	17 F
Valley View. TN4	15 F
Vauxhall La. TN4	14 D
Vermont Rd. TN4	17 F
Vernon Rd. TN1	18 D
Vicarage Rd. TN4	15 E
Victoria Rd. TN4	14 D
Victoria Rd. TN4	3 C
Wallace Clo. TN2	23 E
Wallers. TN3	17 E
Walnut Way. TN4	15 H
Warwick Pk. TN2	3 A
Warwick Rd. TN1	3 B
Waterdown Rd. TN4	22 C
Waterfield. TN2	23 H
Waverley Rd. TN4	19 H
Weare Rd. TN4	15 G
Welbeck Av. TN4	15 G
Weller Rd. TN4	17 F
West Park Av. TN4	15 E
Westbrook Ter. TN2	23 H

Western Rd. TN4 — 15 E5
Western Rd. TN1 — 18 D3
Westway. TN2 — 21 F4
Westwood Rd. TN4 — 17 F4
Whitefield Rd. TN4 — 18 B3
Whitegate Clo. TN4 — 15 E6
Whybourne Crest. TN2 — 23 H4
Wickham Gdns. TN4 — 17 F4
Widbury. TN3 — 16 C5
William St. TN4 — 18 B3
Willow Tree Rd. TN2 — 22 D4
Willow Walk. TN2 — 19 F1
Wilman Rd. TN4 — 18 C2
Wiltshire Way. TN2 — 19 E1
Windmill St. TN2 — 18 D5
Winston Scott Av. TN3 — 16 B5
Wolseley Rd. TN4 — 18 D1
Wood St. TN1 — 3 D14
Woodbury Park Gdns. TN4 — 18 E5
Woodbury Park Rd. TN4 — 18 E5
Woodhill Pk. TN2 — 21 E5
Woodland Rd. TN4 — 18 D1
Woodland Way. TN4 — 14 B3
Woodlands Clo. TN4 — 18 D1
Woodsgate Way. TN2 — 21 E5
Woodside Clo. TN2 — 21 G5
Woodside Rd, Pembury. TN2 — 21 G5
Woodside Rd, Rusthall. TN4 — 17 G4
Wooley Clo. TN4 — 14 D5
Wooley Rd. TN4 — 14 D5
Wybourn Rise. TN2 — 23 G5

Yew Tree Rd. TN4 — 15 E5
York Rd. TN1 — 3 A2

CRANBROOK

Angley Rd. TN17 — 6 A4
Angley Walk. TN17 — 6 C2
Bakers Cross. TN17 — 6 C4
Bank St. TN17 — 6 B4
Bramley Rd. TN17 — 6 C5
Brickenden Rd.TN17 — 6 C5
Broadcloth. TN17 — 6 C5
Brookside. TN17 — 6 C4
Carriers Rd. TN17 — 6 C3
Causton Rd. TN17 — 6 B4
Crane La. TN17 — 6 C4
Dobells Dri. TN17 — 6 C4
Dorothy Av. TN17 — 6 C5
Frythe Clo. TN17 — 6 C5
Frythe Cres. TN17 — 6 C5
Frythe Walk. TN17 — 6 C5
Frythe Way. TN17 — 6 C5
Goddards Clo. TN17 — 6 A5
Golford Rd. TN17 — 6 D4
Goudhurst Rd. TN17 — 6 C1
Greenway. TN17 — 6 A4
Hawkhurst Rd. TN17 — 6 A5
Hendley Dri. TN17 — 6 B4
High St. TN17 — 6 A4
Hopes Rd. TN17 — 6 C4
Huntingdon Clo, Brickenden Rd. TN17 — 6 C4
Imber Ct. TN17 — 6 C4
Jockey La. TN17 — 6 C3
Joyce Clo. TN17 — 6 B4
Kirby Clo. TN17 — 6 C5
New Rd. TN17 — 6 A4
Norman Rise. TN17 — 6 C5
Oatfield Clo. TN17 — 6 B3
Oatfield Dri. TN17 — 6 B3
Orchard Way. TN17 — 6 A5
Pear Tree Clo. TN17 — 6 C5
Pennyfields. TN17 — 6 C5
Quakers Dri. TN17 — 6 C2
Quakers La. TN17 — 6 C2
Rectory Fields. TN17 — 6 C3
Rope Walk. TN17 — 6 B4
St Dunstans Walk. TN17 — 6 C4
Sheafe Dri. TN17 — 6 B4
Stone St. TN17 — 6 C4
Swifts Vw. TN17 — 6 C2
The Crest. TN17 — 6 C4
The Hill. TN17 — 6 C4
The Tanyard. TN17 — 6 C4
Tippens Clo. TN17 — 6 C4
Tower Meadow. TN17 — 6 C4
Turnden. TN17 — 6 A5
Turner Av. TN17 — 6 C5
Waterloo Rd. TN17 — 6 B4
Wheatfield Clo. TN17 — 6 B4
Wheatfield Dri. TN17 — 6 B4
Wheatfield Lea. TN17 — 6 B3
Wheatfield Way. TN17 — 6 B4
Willesley Gdns. TN17 — 6 C2
Winch Clo. TN17 — 6 C5

CROWBOROUGH

Alderbrook Clo. TN6 — 26 C3
Alderbrook Way. TN6 — 26 C3
Aldervale Cotts. TN6 — 26 C3
Alice Bright La. TN6 — 26 B3
April Ct. TN6 — 25 H6
Aviemore Rd. TN6 — 24 B4
Badgers Clo. TN6 — 24 C3
Barnfield. TN6 — 25 E4
Beacon Clo. TN6 — 24 C4
Beacon Gdns. TN6 — 24 C3
Beacon Rd. TN6 — 24 A6
Beacon Rd West. TN6 — 24 B4
Beaver Clo. TN6 — 25 E5
Beeches Farm Rd. TN6 — 25 E5
Beeches Rd. TN6 — 25 E5
Belvedere Gdns. TN6 — 25 E6
Bentley Path. TN6 — 26 E2
Birches Clo. TN6 — 24 D2
Blackness Rd. TN6 — 25 E6
Blacknest. TN6 — 25 E6
Booker Clo. TN6 — 25 E5
Bracken Clo. TN6 — 25 G5
Bramble Croft. TN6 — 25 E4
Brickmead. TN6 — 25 E5
Bridger Way. TN6 — 26 C1
Brincliffe. TN6 — 24 D3
Broadway. TN6 — 24 D3
Brook Clo. TN6 — 25 G5
Brook Ter. TN6 — 24 B2
Brook View. TN6 — 24 B2
Brooklands Av. TN6 — 26 B2
Bryants Fields. TN6 — 24 C3
Buller Clo. TN6 — 26 C1
Burdett Rd. TN6 — 25 G6
Charity Farm Way. TN6 — 25 E3
Chequers Clo. TN6 — 25 E4
Chequers Way. TN6 — 25 E4
Church Rd. TN6 — 24 C4
Clackhams La. TN6 — 26 F2
Clifford Ct. TN6 — 24 D4
Coldharbour Clo. TN6 — 24 D5
Coldharbour Cotts. TN6 — 24 D6
Combe End. TN6 — 24 C6
Common Wood Rise. TN6 — 24 D2
Coopers La. TN6 — 24 B2
Coopers Wood. TN6 — 24 C2
Cornford Clo. TN6 — 24 D5
Croft Rd. TN6 — 24 D4
Croham Rd. TN6 — 24 D4
Crowborough Hill. TN6 — 24 D4
Dodds Hill. TN6 — 25 E5
Deerholm. TN6 — 26 C2
East Beeches Rd. TN6 — 24 D4
Elim Court Gdns. TN6 — 24 C2
Eridge Dri. TN6 — 25 E3
Eridge Gdns. TN6 — 25 E3
Eridge Rd. TN6 — 24 D3
Fairview Cotts. TN6 — 24 C2
Fairview La. TN6 — 24 C2
Farningham Rd. TN6 — 25 G6
Fermor Rd. TN6 — 26 B2
Fermor Row. TN6 — 24 D6
Fermor Way. TN6 — 24 D6
Fernbank Centre. TN6 — 24 B6
Fielden La. TN6 — 24 B6
Fielden Rd. TN6 — 24 B6
Figg La. TN6 — 24 D6
Forest Dene. TN6 — 25 G6
Forest Pk. TN6 — 24 B4
Forest Rise. TN6 — 25 G5
Ghyll Rd. TN6 — 24 C2
Gilridge Grn. TN6 — 24 C2
Gladstone Rd. TN6 — 24 D5
Glenmore Rd. TN6 — 24 A3
Glenmore Rd East. TN6 — 24 B3
Goldsmith Av. TN6 — 24 C3
Gordon Rd. TN6 — 24 D4
Grange Clo. TN6 — 24 C5
Graycoats Dri. TN6 — 24 D4
Green La. TN6 — 25 F4
Green Rd. TN6 — 24 D5
Harecombe Rise. TN6 — 24 C6
Harecombe Rd. TN6 — 24 C6
Harlequin La. TN6 — 24 C6
Harlequin Pl. TN6 — 24 C6
Heather Walk. TN6 — 25 G6
Heavegate Rd. TN6 — 24 A5
Herne Down. TN6 — 26 B2
Herne Rd. TN6 — 24 D6
High Broom La. TN6 — 26 A3
High Broom Rd. TN6 — 26 A2
High Cross Flds. TN6 — 24 D3
High St. TN6 — 24 D3
Highlands Clo. TN6 — 24 C3
Hilders Farm Clo. TN6 — 25 F5
Hill Clo. TN6 — 24 C5
Hill Rise. TN6 — 25 F4
Hoadleys La. TN6 — 24 B1
Hookswood Clo. TN6 — 25 E3
Huntingdon Rd. TN6 — 24 D6
Hurtis Hill. TN6 — 26 A2
Hydehurst Clo. TN6 — 24 D5
INDUSTRIAL ESTATES:
Lexden Lodge Ind Est. TN6 — 25 G6
Millbrook Business Park. TN6 — 25 H6
Inhams Wood. TN6 — 24 C2
Jardine Ct. TN6 — 24 D4
Jefferies Way. TN6 — 24 D2
Kemps Farm Rd. TN6 — 25 E6
Kings Chase. TN6 — 24 C3
Kings Court. TN6 — 24 C4
Knowle Clo. TN6 — 26 E2
Knowle Pk. TN6 — 24 B4
Lexden Lodge Ind Est. TN6 — 25 G6
Links Clo. TN6 — 24 B4
Little Paddocks. TN6 — 24 C5
Little Sunnyside. TN6 — 24 D5
London Rd. TN6 — 24 C1
Lordswell La. TN6 — 24 C6
Lower Saxonbury. TN6 — 24 D4
Loxfield Gdns. TN6 — 25 F5
Luxford Dri. TN6 — 26 C2
Luxford La. TN6 — 26 C1
Luxford Rd. TN6 — 26 C2
Manor Way. TN6 — 24 C6
Mardens Hill. TN6 — 24 A1
Maynards Mead. TN6 — 25 H6
Medway. TN6 — 25 F5
Melfort Rd. TN6 — 24 B5
Mill Cres. TN6 — 24 D3
Mill Dri. TN6 — 24 D4
Mill La. TN6 — 24 C4
Millbrook Business Park. TN6 — 25 H6
Millbrook Rd. TN6 — 25 E3
Montargis Way. TN6 — 24 D5
Mottins Hill. TN6 — 26 F2
Mount Pleasant. TN6 — 26 E2
Myrtle Rd. TN6 — 24 D5
Nevill Rd. TN6 — 24 D3
New Rd. TN6 — 24 D3
Norbury Clo. TN6 — 24 C2
North Beeches Rd. TN6 — 25 E5
Nye Clo. TN6 — 24 D5
Oakhurst Dri. TN6 — 25 E3
Oaklands. TN6 — 25 E5
Ockley Rd. TN6 — 24 A4
Old La, Blacknest. TN6 — 25 F5
Old La, St. Johns. TN6 — 24 B3
Oliver Clo. TN6 — 25 E5
Osborne Hill. TN6 — 25 G6
Osborne Rd. TN6 — 25 F6
Palesgate La. TN6 — 25 F3
Park Cres. TN6 — 24 D3
Park La. TN6 — 24 D3
Park Rd. TN6 — 24 D3
Pilmer Rd. TN6 — 24 D3
Pine Gro. TN6 — 24 C4
Pinewood Chase. TN6 — 24 B3
Pleasant View Rd. TN6 — 24 D2
Poundfield Rd. TN6 — 25 F4
Pratts Folly La. TN6 — 24 C5
Queens Rd. TN6 — 24 D6
Rannoch Rd West. TN6 — 24 B4
Rannoch Rd. TN6 — 24 B4
Rochester Way. TN6 — 25 F5
Rockingham Way. TN6 — 26 D1
Rodwell. TN6 — 25 G6
Rother Clo. TN6 — 26 C2
Rotherfield Rd. TN6 — 26 F2
Rotherhill Rd. TN6 — 24 C6
St Denys View. TN6 — 25 E3
St Johns Clo. TN6 — 24 C5
St Johns Rd. TN6 — 24 B2
St Michaels Clo. TN6 — 26 D1
St Richards Rd. TN6 — 26 C2
Sandridge. TN6 — 24 C5
Saxonbury Clo. TN6 — 24 D4
School La. TN6 — 24 D5
School La, St. Johns. TN6 — 24 B2
Sefton Chase. TN6 — 25 E3
Sefton Way. TN6 — 25 E3
Shaw Field. TN6 — 25 F5
Sheep Plain. TN6 — 24 B6
Sheiling Rd. TN6 — 24 C3
Shepherds Walk. TN6 — 25 F5
Simons Clo. TN6 — 25 E5
Smugglers La. TN6 — 24 B5
South St. TN6 — 24 D5
Southridge Rise. TN6 — 24 C6
Southridge Rd. TN6 — 24 C6
Southview Clo. TN6 — 24 C5
Southview Rd. TN6 — 24 C6
Springfield Clo. TN6 — 25 F4
Springhead Way. TN6 — 24 C6
Starfield. TN6 — 24 C6
Station Rd. TN6 — 25 G6
Stone Cross Rd. TN6 — 26 B3
Stonecott Clo. TN6 — 24 D6
Swaylands Av. TN6 — 26 B2
Swift Clo. TN6 — 24 B5
Sybron Way. TN6 — 25 H6
Tanners Way. TN6 — 25 E5
The Close. TN6 — 24 C3
The Farthings. TN6 — 25 E3
The Glebelands. TN6 — 24 D4
The Green. TN6 — 24 D4
The Grove. TN6 — 24 C5
The Martlets. TN6 — 24 D4
The Meadows. TN6 — 24 D4
The Park. TN6 — 24 D5
The Twitten. TN6 — 24 C5
Tollwood Pk. TN6 — 25 F5
Tollwood Rd. TN6 — 25 F6
Treblers Rd. TN6 — 26 F2
Trenches Rd. TN6 — 24 D5
Troy Clo. TN6 — 24 D5
Tubwell La. TN6 — 26 F2
Twyfords. TN6 — 24 C5
Valley Rd. TN6 — 24 D4
Valley View Clo. TN6 — 24 D5
Victoria Rd. TN6 — 25 G6
Wallis Clo. TN6 — 26 C1
Walshes Rd. TN6 — 26 C3
Warren Gdns. TN6 — 24 C4
Warren Rd. TN6 — 24 A5
Wealden Clo. TN6 — 24 D3
Wellesley Clo. TN6 — 24 B5
Wesley Mews. TN6 — 24 D4
West Beeches Rd. TN6 — 25 E5
West Way. TN6 — 24 C2
Western Gdns. TN6 — 26 F2
Western Rd. TN6 — 26 E2
Whincroft Pk. TN6 — 24 B6
White Hill Clo. TN6 — 24 D5
Whitehill Rd. TN6 — 24 D5
Wilderness Park. TN6 — 24 C4
Willowmead. TN6 — 26 A2
Windsor Pl. TN6 — 25 G6
Windsor Rd. TN6 — 25 G6
Wolfe Clo. TN6 — 25 G6
Woodland Way. TN6 — 26 B2
Woodside. TN6 — 24 C4

EAST PECKHAM

Addlestead Rd. TN12 — 31 B5
Arnold Business Pk. TN12 — 31 D5
Bardsley Clo. TN12 — 31 C4
Barnfield. TN12 — 31 C4
Bramley Rd. TN12 — 31 B5
Branbridges Ind Est. TN12 — 31 D6
Branbridges Rd. TN12 — 31 D5
Bullen La. TN12 — 31 A4
Bush Rd. TN12 — 31 A5
Caysers Croft. TN12 — 31 A5
Chidley Cross Rd. TN12 — 31 B5
Church La. TN12 — 31 B4
Cotman Way. TN12 — 31 B5
Crown Acres. TN12 — 31 C5
Drage Rd. TN12 — 31 C5
Fell Mead. TN12 — 31 B5
Freehold. TN12 — 31 C5
Golding Gdns. TN12 — 31 C5
Hale Ct. TN12 — 31 D4
Hale St. TN12 — 31 C4
Hatches La. TN12 — 31 A5
Henham Gdns. TN12 — 31 C5
INDUSTRIAL ESTATES:
Arnold Business Pk. TN12 — 31 D5
Branbridges Ind Est. TN12 — 31 D6
Marvillion Ct. TN12 — 31 C5
Medway Meadows. TN12 — 31 D5
Old Rd. TN12 — 31 C5
Orchard Rd. TN12 — 31 C5
Pattenden Gdns. TN12 — 31 D4
Pinkham. TN12 — 31 C6
Pinkham Gdns. TN12 — 31 C5
Pippin Rd. TN12 — 31 B5
Pound Rd. TN12 — 31 B4
Russet Rd. TN12 — 31 B5
Smithers Ct. TN12 — 31 D4
Smithers La. TN12 — 31 D4
Snoll Hatch Rd. TN12 — 31 B6
Stockenbury. TN12 — 31 B5
Strettit Gdns. TN12 — 31 C5
Tonbridge Rd. TN12 — 31 A6
Torbay Rd. TN12 — 31 D6
Westwood Rd. TN12 — 31 B5
Whitebine Gdns. TN12 — 31 C5
William Luck Clo. TN12 — 31 B5

EDENBRIDGE

Albion Way. TN8 — 4 B2
Ash Clo. TN8 — 4 B5
Ashcombe Dri. TN8 — 4 B1
Barnhawe. TN8 — 4 B4
Briar Clo. TN8 — 4 C3
Cedar Dri. TN8 — 4 B3
Chestnut Clo. TN8 — 4 B4
Church Field. TN8 — 4 C5
Church St. TN8 — 4 C5
Clover Walk. TN8 — 4 C3
Commerce Way. TN8 — 4 B3
Coomb Field. TN8 — 4 B5
Croft Clo. TN8 — 4 C4
Croft La. TN8 — 4 C4
Crouch House Rd. TN8 — 4 A2
Crown Rd. TN8 — 4 C2
Enterprise Way. TN8 — 4 B2
Enterprise Way Ind Est. TN8 — 4 B2
Fairmead Rd. TN8 — 4 B1
Farmstead Dri. TN8 — 4 C3
Field Dri. TN8 — 4 C2
Fircroft Way. TN8 — 4 B2
Fircroft Way Ind Est. TN8 — 4 C3
Forge Croft. TN8 — 4 C4
Four Elms Rd. TN8 — 4 B3
Foxglove Clo. TN8 — 4 C3
Frant Field. TN8 — 4 C4
Grange Clo. TN8 — 4 C4
Great Mead. TN8 — 4 B3
Greenfield. TN8 — 4 B4
Halland Ct. TN8 — 4 B4
Harrow Clo. TN8 — 4 C3
Hawthorn Clo. TN8 — 4 B3
Heron Clo. TN8 — 4 C3
Hever Rd. TN8 — 4 C5
Hever Rd Ind Park. TN8 — 4 C6
High Fields Rd. TN8 — 4 B1
High St. TN8 — 4 B4
Hilders Clo. TN8 — 4 B1
Hilders La. TN8 — 4 A2
Hillcrest Rd. TN8 — 4 B1
Homestead Rd. TN8 — 4 B1
Hopgarden Clo. TN8 — 4 C3
INDUSTRIAL ESTATES:
Enterprise Way Ind Est. TN8 — 4 B2
Fircroft Way Ind Est. TN8 — 4 C3
Hever Rd Ind Pk. TN8 — 4 C6
Katherine Rd. TN8 — 4 C3
Kestrel Clo. TN8 — 4 C3
Leathermarket. TN8 — 4 C5
Lingfield Rd. TN8 — 4 A5
Lucilina Dri. TN8 — 4 B5
Lynmead Clo. TN8 — 4 B1
Magpie Green. TN8 — 4 C3
Main Rd. TN8 — 4 B1
Mallard Way. TN8 — 4 C3
Manor House Gdns. TN8 — 4 B4
Manor Rd. TN8 — 4 B5
Marl Hurst. TN8 — 4 B2
Marlpit Clo. TN8 — 4 B2
Mead Rd. TN8 — 4 C6
Meadow La. TN8 — 4 B2
Mill Hill. TN8 — 4 C6
New House Ter. TN8 — 4 B3
Oakfield Rd. TN8 — 4 B1
Orchard Clo. TN8 — 4 A3
Orchard Dri. TN8 — 4 A3
Oxfield. TN8 — 4 C3
Park Av. TN8 — 4 B3
Park View. TN8 — 4 B4
Penlee Clo. TN8 — 4 B4
Pine Gro. TN8 — 4 B4
Pit La. TN8 — 4 B3
Plough Walk. TN8 — 4 C3
Plover Clo. TN8 — 4 C3
Queens Ct. TN8 — 4 C4

Ridge Way. TN8   4 C2
Riverside. TN8   4 C5
Riverside Ct. TN8   4 C5
Robyns Way. TN8   4 C5
Rowfield. TN8   4 C3
Skeynes Pk. TN8   4 A5
Skeynes Rd. TN8   4 B5
Skinners La. TN8   4 C3
Smithyfield. TN8   4 C3
Sorrell Clo. TN8   4 C5
Spital Cross Est. TN8   4 C3
Springfield Rd. TN8   4 B5
Stackfield. TN8   4 C3
Stanbridge Rd. TN8   4 B4
Stangrove Rd. TN8   4 B4
Station App. TN8   4 C4
Station Rd. TN8   4 B2
Stoneyfield. TN8   4 C3
Streatfeild. TN8   4 C5
Sunnyside. TN8   4 B2
Swan La. TN8   4 B1
Swan Ridge. TN8   4 C2
The Brownings. TN8   4 B1
The Limes. TN8   4 B5
The Plat. TN8   4 C5
The Square. TN8   4 C5
Victoria Clo. TN8   4 C6
Victoria Rd. TN8   4 C6
Wainhouse Clo. TN8   4 C3
Water Lakes. TN8   4 C6
Wayside Dri. TN8   4 C3
Westways. TN8   4 B3
Woodland Dri. TN8   4 C3
Woodpecker Clo. TN8   4 C3

FOREST ROW

Allens Clo. RH19   27 B1
Ashdown Clo. RH18   27 D5
Ashdown Rd. RH18   27 C5
Balfour Gdns. RH18   27 C6
Beeches La. RH19   27 A1
Blacklands Cres. RH18   27 D5
Blenheim Fields. RH18   27 C4
Box La. RH19   27 B1
Broadstone. RH18   27 D5
Cansiron La. RH19   27 C1
Chapel La,
  Ashurstwood. RH19   27 B1
Chapel La,
  Forest Row. RH18   27 D6
Chequer Clo. RH18   27 C5
Colchester Vale. RH18   27 B5
Dale Rd. RH18   27 C5
Dirty La. RH19   27 B1
Forest Row Business
  Park. RH18   27 D4
Freshfield Bank. RH18   27 B5
Gage Ridge. RH18   27 B5
Gilham La. RH18   27 C4
Hammerwood Rd. RH19   27 B1
Hartfield Rd. RH18   27 C4
Hatch End. RH18   27 C5
Highfields. RH18   27 C5
Highgate Rd. RH18   27 C6
INDUSTRIAL ESTATES:
  Forest Row Business
  Park. RH18   27 D4
Ink Pen La. RH18   27 C6
Ivy Dene La. RH19   27 A1
Kidbrooke Rise. RH18   27 B5
Lewes Rd,
  Ashurstwood. RH19   27 A1
Lewes Rd,
  Forest Row. RH18   27 B6
Lower Rd. RH18   27 C4
Maypole Rd. RH18   27 B1
Medway Dri. RH18   27 D5
Medway View. RH18   27 D5
Michael Fields. RH18   27 B5

Newlands Pl. RH18   27 C4
Oakwood Park. RH18   27 C5
Park Cres. RH18   27 D5
Park La. RH19   27 A1
Park Rd. RH18   27 B5
Phoenix La. RH19   27 B1
Post Horn La. RH18   27 D5
Primrose La. RH18   27 D6
Priory Rd. RH18   27 B5
Riverside. RH18   27 B4
School La,
  Ashurstwood. RH19   27 B1
School La,
  Forest Row. RH18   27 C5
Shalesbrook La. RH18   27 D6
Spring Meadows. RH18   27 C6
Station Rd. RH18   27 C5
Stonedene Clo. RH18   27 D5
Stonepark Dri. RH18   27 D5
Swans Ghyll. RH18   23 C4
Tompsets Bank. RH18   27 C6
Upper Clo. RH18   27 C5
Upper Hillside
  Square. RH18   27 C4
Wall Hill Rd. RH19   27 A1
Woodcote Rd. RH18   27 C5
Woods Hill Clo. RH19   27 A1
Woods Hill La. RH18   27 A1
Wray Clo. RH19   27 B1

GROOMBRIDGE

Birchden Rd. TN3   30 C4
Bird in Hand Hill. TN3   30 B1
Broad Oak. TN3   30 C3
Corseley Rd. TN3   30 C3
Florence La. TN3   30 B3
Gromenfield. TN3   30 C3
Groombridge Hill. TN3   30 C2
Lealands Clo. TN3   30 C3
Liendell Hill. TN3   30 A4
Meadow Rd. TN3   30 C3
New Dri. TN3   30 A4
Newton Willows. TN3   30 C3
Oaklands Rd. TN3   30 B3
Orchard Rise. TN3   30 B3
Springfield Rd. TN3   30 C3
Station Rd. TN3   30 B3
Tanyard Hill. TN3   30 B4
The Close. TN3   30 C3
The Walks. TN3   30 B1
Wallis Field. TN3   30 B3
Withyham Rd. TN3   30 A3

HAWKHURST

All Saints Rd. TN18   30 C6
Barretts Rd. TN18   30 B5
Basden Cotts. TN18   30 B6
Copthall Av. TN18   30 B6
Cranbrook Rd. TN18   30 B5
Dickens Way. TN18   30 C6
Dunlop Ct. TN18   30 C5
Eden Ct. TN18   30 B5
Fairview. TN18   30 B6
Fieldways. TN18   30 C6
Hammonds. TN18   30 B5
Hartnokes. TN18   30 C5
Heartenoak Rd. TN18   30 C5
High St. TN18   30 A5
Highfield Clo. TN18   30 C6
Highgate Hill. TN18   30 B6
Mercers. TN18   30 B6
Murton Neale Clo. TN18   30 C5
Northgrove Rd. TN18   30 B5
Oakfield. TN18   30 B5
Oaklands Rd. TN18   30 B6
Ockley La. TN18   30 B5

Ockley Rd. TN18   30 B5
Park Cotts. TN18   30 C5
Queens Ct. TN18   30 C5
Queens Rd. TN18   30 C5
Rye Rd. TN18   30 C6
School Ter. TN18   30 B5
Slip Mill Rd. TN18   30 A5
Sopers Rd. TN18   30 A5
Tates. TN18   30 B6
The Colonnade. TN18   30 B5
The Smugglers. TN18   30 C6
Theobalds. TN18   30 B5
Vale Rd. TN18   30 B5
Water La. TN18   30 D6
Western Av. TN18   30 B5
Western Rd. TN18   30 C5
Whites La. TN18   30 C5
Winchester Rd. TN18   30 B5
Woodbury Rd. TN18   30 B5

HORSMONDEN

Angley Ct. TN12   31 C3
Back La. TN12   31 C2
Brenchley Rd. TN12   31 A3
Fromandez Dr. TN12   31 B2
Furnace La. TN12   31 B1
Gibbet La. TN12   31 B2
Goudhurst Rd. TN12   31 C3
Gunlands. TN12   31 C2
Haymans Hill. TN12   31 D1
Heath Ter. TN12   31 C2
Hoath Mdw. TN12   31 C2
Kirkins Clo. TN12   31 C2
Lamberhurst Rd. TN12   31 B3
Maidstone Rd. TN12   31 C2
Morley Dri. TN12   31 B2
Oast View. TN12   31 C2
Orchard Clo. TN12   31 B2
Orchard Cres. TN12   31 C2
Orchard Way. TN12   31 C2
The Green. TN12   31 C2
The Mannerings. TN12   31 C2

PADDOCK WOOD

Acorn Clo. TN12   28 B3
Alders Cotts. TN12   28 A5
Alders Rd. TN12   28 A5
Alliance Wy. TN12   29 E4
Allington Rd. TN12   29 E3
Apple Ct. TN12   29 E4
Ashcroft Rd. TN12   29 F5
Badsell Rd. TN12   28 C4
Ballard Way. TN12   29 G3
Birch Rd. TN12   29 F4
Bowls Pl. TN12   29 F3
Bramley Gdns. TN12   29 E3
Bridge Business Park.
  TN12   28 C2
Bullfinch Clo. TN12   29 F5
Bullion Clo. TN12   29 E4
Catts Pl. TN12   29 H6
Chaffinch Way. TN12   29 F5
Challenger Clo. TN12   29 E4
Chantlers Hill. TN12   29 F6
Church La. TN12   28 A5
Church Rd. TN12   29 F3
Claverdell Rd. TN12   29 F3
Cobbs Clo. TN12   29 E4
Cogate Rd. TN12   29 E4
Colts Hill. TN12   28 B6
Colts Hill Pl. TN12   28 B5
Commercial Rd. TN12   29 F4
Concord Clo. TN12   29 E3
Court Hope. TN12   29 F4
Crittenden La. TN12   28 B6
Dimmock Clo. TN12   29 G4

Eastlands. TN12   29 E2
Eastwell Clo. TN12   29 E4
Eldon Way. TN12   29 E3
Eldon Way Ind Est.
  TN12   29 E3
Evens Clo. TN12   29 F4
Falmouth Pl. TN12   28 B3
Five Oak Green Rd.
  TN12   28 A3
Forest Rd. TN12   29 F4
Forge Way. TN12   29 F3
Fuggles Clo. TN12   29 E4
Goldfinch Clo. TN12   29 F5
Goldings. TN12   29 E5
Granary. TN12   29 G4
Haywain Clo. TN12   29 F5
Henley Rd. TN12   29 F3
Hop Pocket La. TN12   29 F3
Hoppers. TN12   28 B3
Hornbeam Clo. TN12   29 F5
INDUSTRIAL ESTATES:
  Bridge Business Park.
  TN12   28 C2
  Eldon Way Ind Est.
  TN12   29 E3
  Paddock Wood Distribution
  Centre. TN12   29 G3
  Transfesa. TN12   29 G3
Kent Clo. TN12   29 F4
Keyworth Clo. TN12   29 E4
Kiln Way. TN12   29 E4
Larch Gro. TN12   29 F4
Larkfield. TN12   28 B3
Laxton Gdns. TN12   29 E4
Le Temple Rd. TN12   29 G4
Linden Clo. TN12   29 F5
Linnet Way. TN12   29 F5
Lucknow Rd. TN12   29 F3
Lucks La. TN12   29 G2
Macdonald Ct. TN12   29 F4
Maidstone Rd, Five Oak
  Green. TN12   28 C4
Maidstone Rd, Paddock
  Wood. TN12   29 F2
Mascalls Ct Rd. TN12   29 F6
Mascalls Park. TN12   29 E5
Mercers Clo. TN12   29 E4
Mile Oak Rd. TN12   29 H6
Mount Pleasant. TN12   29 E4
New Rd. TN12   29 F4
Newton Gdns. TN12   29 E3
North Down Clo. TN12   29 E4
Nortons Way. TN12   28 A3
Nursery Rd. TN12   29 F3
Oak Rd. TN12   28 B3
Oaklea Rd. TN12   29 F4
Old Kent Rd. TN12   29 F4
Paddock Wood Distribution
  Centre. TN12   29 G3
Pearsons Green Rd.
  TN12   29 H5
Pemble Clo. TN12   28 B3
Pinewood Clo. TN12   29 F4
Queen St. TN12   29 H5
Redpoll Walk. TN12   29 F5
Redwood Pk. TN12   28 A5
Ribston Gdns. TN12   29 E3
Ringden Av. TN12   29 E5
Rowan Clo. TN12   29 F5
St Andrews Clo. TN12   29 F4
St Andrews Rd. TN12   29 F4
Siskin Gdns. TN12   29 F5
Staces Cotts. TN12   29 H5
Station App. TN12   29 F3
Station R. TN12   29 F3
Sycamore Gdns. TN12   29 F5
Sychem La. TN12   28 B3
Sychem Pl. TN12   28 A3
The Cedars. TN12   29 F3
The Greenways. TN12   29 E5
The Ridings. TN12   29 F3

The Shires. TN12   29 G3
Tolhurst Rd. TN12   28 B3
Transfesa. TN12   29 G3
Transfesa Rd. TN12   29 F2
Tutsham Way. TN12   29 E4
Wagon La. TN12   29 G1
Walnut Clo. TN12   29 F4
Warrington Rd. TN12   29 F4
Whetsted Rd. TN12   28 B3
Willow Cres. TN12   28 B3
Woodlands. TN12   29 E3
Yeoman Gdns. TN12   29 E4

WADHURST

Balaclava La. TN5   5 C2
Baldock Rd. TN5   5 A4
Bankside. TN5   5 B4
Bassetts Forge. TN5   5 B4
Bayham Ct. TN5   5 B3
Blacksmith La. TN5   5 D5
Bocking Clo. TN5   5 B5
Brinkers La. TN5   5 D6
Castle Walk. TN5   5 B5
Church St. TN5   5 C5
Cockmount La. TN5   5 B4
Courthope Av. TN5   5 C5
Crittles Ct. TN5   5 C5
Deepdene. TN5   5 B4
Durgates Ind. Est. TN5   5 B4
Fuller Clo. TN5   5 B4
George St. TN5   5 C3
Gloucester Rd. TN5   5 B3
Green Sq. TN5   5 C4
High St. TN5   5 C4
Highbury Pl. TN5   5 C4
Hollydene Rd. TN5   5 C5
Holmsdale Clo. TN5   5 B4
INDUSTRIAL ESTATES:
  Durgates Ind. Est. TN5   5 B4
Jonas Dri. TN5   5 B4
Jonas La. TN5   5 B4
Kingsley Ct. TN5   5 D5
Lamberhurst Rd. TN5   5 C4
Little Park. TN5   5 F4
Mayfield La. TN5   5 A5
Mayfield Park. TN5   5 A4
Mount Pleasant. TN5   5 B3
Old Station Rd. TN5   5 B3
Osmers Hill. TN5   5 C2
Pell Clo. TN5   5 D3
Pell Hill. TN5   5 D3
Primmers Grn Rd. TN5   5 C3
Queens Cotts. TN5   5 B3
Snape View. TN5   5 C5
South View Rd. TN5   5 C3
Southfields. TN5   5 C3
Sparrows Grn. TN5   5 B4
Station Rd. TN5   5 A3
Stonebridge La. TN5   5 B2
Stonecross Rd. TN5   5 D5
Tapsells La. TN5   5 A4
The Leas. TN5   5 B4
The Marlpit. TN5   5 B4
The Square. TN5   5 D5
Three Oaks La. TN5   5 A2
Townlands Rd. TN5   5 C5
Turners Green La. TN5   5 C2
Turners Green Rd. TN5   5 C2
Vicarage La. TN5   5 D4
Ward Clo. TN5   5 B5
Washwell La. TN5   5 C6
Waters Cotts. TN5   5 D5
Watts Clo. TN5   5 C5
Weald View. TN5   5 C3
Wellington Pl. TN5   5 C4
Western Rd. TN5   5 B3
Whitegate La. TN5   5 A1
Windmill La. TN5   5 A5
Wyck La. TN5   5 C1

Edition 009L 1.97.